STRUCTURE OF URBAN POVERTY

STRUCTURE OF URBAN POVERTY

The Case of Bombay Slums

S.S.JHA

BOMBAY
POPULAR PRAKASHAN

POPULAR PRAKASHAN PRIVATE LIMITED

35-C, Pandit Madan Mohan Malaviya Marg,
Popular Press Bldg., Opp. "Roche", Tardeo, Bombay 400 034

First published 1986

© S.S. JHA, 1986

(3348)

ISBN   0 86132 134 0

Printed in India

by R.K. Dhawan at Dhawan Printing Works, A-26 Mayapuri, Phase I, New
Delhi 110 064 and published by Ramdas Bhatkal for Popular Prakashan,
Pvt. Ltd., 35-C, Pandit Madan Mohan Malaviya Marg, Tardeo
Bombay 400 034

to

A. R. DESAI

my teacher, my friend

PREFACE

A few years ago the Indian Council of Social Science Research, New Delhi, provided me with funds to conduct a field-study on the problems relating to relocation and improvement of slums in Bombay. This book is a product of that work. I am grateful to the ICSSR for sponsoring and funding the project. Without their help and co-operation I would not have been able to complete the work.

The idea of conducting a field-study of this kind and relating it to the poverty question came from Prof. A.R. Desai. My most immediate debt is to him. During the formulation of the research project, Prof. T.S. Papola gave me several suggestions which proved to be highly fruitful. I feel grateful to him.

Among the persons who helped me complete the project work, Shri Colin K. Gonsalves figures prominently. He joined as research officer for a brief period. I benefited greatly from incisive suggestions he gave me at the time of the field work. Later, after leaving the project, he wrote three extremely valuable essays on the slum question in the city of Bombay. This study has drawn extensively on these essays. Very sincerely, I acknowledge his co-operation and record my thanks.

Shri M. Peethambaran replaced Shri Gonsalves as research officer and helped me in organising the data collected and preparing the statistical tables. Shri Arvind Kumar Nagar, Shri Biplab Basu, Mrs. Nirmala Sathe, Ms. Saroj Dharmadhikari and Ms. Suniti S. Sohoni worked on the project as field investigators. All of them demonstrated in ample measure their sincerity of purpose and carried out the arduous task of visiting the slums under study time and again and interviewing the people there. I am very thankful to them indeed. Shri P. Vivek, my Ph.D. student, helped me in a variety of ways while I was preparing the draft of the report. I am deeply thankful to him also. Last but not the least, I am thankful to Shri P.D.Antony for giving me excellent secretarial assistance.

S.S. JHA

CONTENTS

INTRODUCTION

It is stating the obvious that our major metropolitan centres have reached a chocking point. Those who inhabit these prime centres of growth come to realise it at some stage of their everyday existence that these places are at the point of implosion. To quote from a newspaper article, "Their civic infrastructure is crumbling rapidly (if it has not actually collapsed), the quality of their environment is deteriorating to unbearable levels, their transport system has become one vast mess, and their housing problems have become all but insoluble. And they continue to grow, feeding on an endless rural exodus, at what must historically be among the highest rates of expansion anywhere. They can only inflict more misery, hardship and humiliation upon their inhabitants. The poor of India's cities have never had it good. But now, even the middle and upper middle classes are not spared".[1] Water scarcity, ever deteriorating traffic system, acute shortage of schools, public hospitals and other civic amenities and above all the growing intractability of shelter, (even a tiny, decent, tolerable shelter) and urban renewal problems seem to drive these metropolitan centres to the point of self-strangulation.

In the process of this decay those who suffer most are the people inhabiting crumbling chawls, zhuggis, basties and jhopadpatties—the slums of the city. Not only that they live in degrading sub-human (sub-animal is perhaps the correct ex-

1. Praful Bidwai, "Metropolises in Decay", *Times of India*, April 27 1983.

STRUCTURE OF URBAN POVERTY

pression) conditions, they are under constant attack from the governmental and civic authorities. Their most dreaded fear being that they can be uprooted from their existing settlements and thrown out on any day the public authorities desire it to do so. The classic examples are the ruthlessly executed demolition of thousands of hutments extending from Jama Masjid to Turkman Gate in Delhi, and the gun-point eviction of seventy thousand hutment dwellers residing in a slum complex called Janata Colony in Bombay. A process of eviction has been going on unabated in our metropolitan centres for over a decade now. There has been a concerted drive against the pavement and the hutment dwellers of these cities during this period. The city administration and the government, generally do it in the name of relocation and improvement of slums.

Bombay is the biggest growing metropolis functioning as the industrial-commercial capital of the country, where according to one estimate on an average nearly three hundred new persons arrive everyday in search of jobs and with a desire to settle down in the city. According to the latest figures available more than fifty per cent of the city's population live in slums of one kind or the other and on pavements. Vast majority of people migrating to the city are from rural areas—its boundary extending to several states in the country. Acute impoverishment of small farmers and near-hunger situation of landless labour lead mainly to this 'flight' and 'distress' migrations to the city. They come here with little or no savings and they find that the opportunities for regular wage-earning are much fewer than their numbers with the result that most of them occupy the lowest rung of the urban society. The state shows its inability to house these urban poor. Private-builders construct houses for profit and not to house the needy. So these urban poor construct their own dwellings which reflect the deprivation, squalor and degradation of their daily lives. The city continues to be a hostile place for them but as it provides a market for their cheap labour they cling on to the city developing a 'culture of survival'. Thus multiply the slums which contrast so nakedly with the glitter and glamour of the city centres and the affluence of some of its suburbs.[2]

2. Colin Gonsalves, *Bombay: A City under Siege*, ISRE, Bombay, 1981 (see Foreword by Narendra Panjwani).

II

Social scientists' interest in the study of slums emanates mainly from the city-ward migration and the conditions of living of the people. A survey of research done on slums in Indian cities would show that while we have some data providing their social profiles and indicating the magnitude of the problem, we have hardly any research done on the issues and problems ensuing along with the acts of eviction, relocation, improvement and resettlement of the existing slums. The issues which arise out of the resettlement programme can broadly be classified and enumerated as follows:

(i) The suitability, administrative feasibility and convenience, and social and economic effectiveness of the different approaches would differ from one situation to another. For example, if congestion is the major concern, relocation may recommend itself as the suitable way to deal with the slum problem; and if improvement in the quality of slum dweller's life rather than issues such as congestion is the main problem, then improvement of the existing slums may be preferred. In most cases the two types of situations co-exist. Therefore, a careful study of their relative importance may be necessary before deciding upon the approach to be adopted.

(ii) The operational success and subsequent effectiveness of a resettlement programme may depend, to a large extent, on the process of resettlement itself. The major issue in this context is the degree of involvement and participation of those being re-settled under the resettlement programme. Imposition of a programme, however well-meaning, may evoke resistance and non-cooperation from the slum dwellers which may also affect adversely the degree of acceptability of, and satisfaction from, the new environs. The process and strategy of resettlement, therefore, becomes an important element in the programme.

(iii) A resettlement programme does not merely imply provision of new space, houses or facilities but ultimately aims at improvement in the social and economic contents of life. A change in environment disturbs the social equilibrium, and a change of place in the relocation of slums may also involve dislocation of the existing economic activities of the slum dwellers. It is, therefore, very important to study the change that takes place in the lives of the resettled, transplanted and acculturated inhabitants. Further, it is also important to examine whether the relocation or resettlement provides possibility of growth for the community of the rehabilitated or it condemns them to a stagnant isolation increasing the wretchedness of their life. Equally important is to see whether the whole programme of relocation or resettlement is tacitly geared to evicting them from their present place of residence and throwing them out and thus leaving them with no option but to struggle for settlement again in a much worse place and surroundings.

(iv) The urban problem, as it is defined, cannot be viewed in isolation because it does not have an autonomous existence. It is organically linked with the nature of distribution of a city's resources and the ideology of urban planning. It is our common experience that despite several decades of town planning efforts in our country urban environmental and housing situation have continued to worsen. Whether one talks of metropolises, large cities, small cities or towns of different sizes, the overall deterioration over the years, of their environment and living conditions has been the most visible mark of their growth. A close examination, therefore, of housing programmes, distribution of urban resources available to the city authorities, particularly land, and the urban planning processes taken as a whole, becomes imperative for an understanding and identification of the root cause of the urban problem.

III

The urban problem in general and the fast growing slums in particular in Bombay seem to have awakened the government of Maharashtra and the Bombay Civic authorities in early sixties to find solutions to the problem and to contain further growth of slums. A series of Acts have been passed by the State Legislature and the Municipal Corporation in Bombay since then. Some of them have been referred to in the text of this study. Earlier, in the fifties, some slums were demolished and as there was no serious resistance to such acts of the government, the act of such eviction and demolition was without any legal garb was supported by brute police force.

In 1976 a census of the slums of the city was undertaken by the government with a view to identify the slum pockets, to know the total number of slum dwellers in the city, and to locate the types of land these slums occupied like Municipal Corporation land, State Government land, Maharashtra Housing Board land, Central Government land and Private land. It was a single day operation with seven thousand persons engaged to complete the entire enumeration in a few hours. As the report was finalised it came to light that large number of slums were left out of this operation, meaning thereby that people inhabiting these slums existed as illegal occupants of the area in the eyes of the government and the civic authorities. Consequently, they were not only not going to get any benefit out of the proposed amelioration plan like relocation and improvement of slums, they were to be evicted and their 'illegal' structures to be demolished. Lakhs of pavement dwellers were, of course, left out as the government did not consider them as bona fide dwellers of the city.

The present study was undertaken to examine this plan of relocation and improvement of slums as it operated in this metropolis with certain objectives in view as specified below:

(i) to review the slum clearance programme in terms of its planning, execution and approaches;

(ii) to assess the relative operational performance of the 'improvement' and 'relocation' approaches to the slum problem;

(iii) to examine the degree of the slum dweller's co-operation and involvement in different resettlement schemes and analyse their attitudes towards them;

(iv) to assess the effectiveness of resettlement in terms of its impact on the social and economic life of the resettled;

(v) to evolve guidelines for the approaches and the strategies of slum resettlement with a view to improving performance and effectiveness of the resettlement programme.

As the study proceeded it was realised soon that the whole

question of relocation and improvement of slums was vitally and crucially linked with larger questions of the housing policy, nature of the existing land legislations and the city planning policy. As stated above it was realised that the questions of slum re-settlement and slum improvement do not have autonomous existence; they are inextricably linked with the property system obtaining in the city, and, therefore, a complete understanding of this urban problem is possible only in the context of the land system operating in the city and the planning process there. Hence, the scope of this study, was enlarged.

In accordance with the broadened objectives of this study, three broad categories of data were required:

(i) information about the programme: The slum clearance schemes and the slum resettlements, their planning, organisation and administration;

(ii) information relating to the urban housing programme, the land acts, the town planning process, ordinances, enactments, legislations with reference to the slums in Bombay city;

(iii) physical, social, political and economic conditions in the pre-settlement and post-settlement situations; housing and amenities, neighbourhood, community life, tensions, occupations and incomes, preferences and aspirations of the inhabitants and so forth.

For the first two categories of data this study has depended on the secondary sources. Qualitative and quantitative material from official and non-official sources like government reports, 1971 and 1981 Census data on the city, relevant papers presented at different seminars conducted by concerned educational and semi-government institutions and organisations involving the inhabitants of some of the rehabilitated slums etc. were collected and analysed. Some of these sources are published and some remain in mimeographed form.

For the third category of data, an extensive survey among the sample of slum households was conducted. The survey was restricted to four slums, of which one falls in the category of 'relocated' and the rest are treated as 'improved'. The four slums selected for the study were Bharat Nagar of Bandra, Golibar

Colony and Hanuman Tekdi situated along the Western Express Highway and Maya Nagar of Worli. Four hundred interviews were conducted with the help of an interview schedule from the households in the slums randomly selected for the purpose of study.

IV

The text of the study is devoted to the issues pertaining to the development of slums in Bombay, slums and the processes of city planning, the question of housing, and the slum improvement programmes in the city. Findings of the field survey mentioned above are also included in the text.

Incorporated in the section on field study is a separate study of women in the slums surveyed. As stated in the section under the heading 'A Profile of Slums Women', it was realised that slum women tend to have a distinct personality. Economic positions that they find themselves in, the physical space that they share and the social environment that they live in, combine to shape this personality. The study was designed not to test any particular hypothesis, but to obtain information on their social characteristics, to assess their status in their own society, to record the degree of tension, fear and exploitation they undergo and such other questions. One hundred married women randomly selected from all the four slums under study were interviewed with a structured questionnaire for this purpose.

The field study is followed by a chapter narrating the conditions of living in certain demolished, relocated and 'improved' slums and chawls in the city. Some local newspapers have been carrying from time to time the accounts of the slum eviction programme in the city. In these newspaper reports one gets a vivid picture of the wretched conditions in which the evicted slum dwellers live as also the atrocities inflicted upon them by the governmental authorities. Our account here is based entirely on such newspaper reports selected for the purpose and reproduced here to highlight the consequences of thoughtless eviction of slums in the city.

The text of this report ends with our concluding remarks.

Relevant tables of the field study conducted by us are arranged serially and presented in appendix.

STRUCTURE OF URBAN POVERTY

CHAPTER ONE

SLUMS IN BOMBAY: A BRIEF SKETCH

I

Studies on urban development have shown that modern urban slums are an outgrowth of limited and distorted industrial and commercial development and that they punctuate almost every city in the world. Countries which have followed the path of development based on privately-owned means of production have always ended up with vast areas of stink, misery, squalor and degradation for the poor and bulk of middle class inhabitants of their cities. In contrast, countries which have succeeded in breaking through this matrix by freeing land, construction and habitation from the orbit of anarchy and exploitative market operations, have also succeeded in eliminating slums in a planned manner. Slums in the cities of such countries, as it shows today, have become a part of the tragic past.

As there is industrial and commercial expansion in cities, people migrate from nearby and far-off areas to such cities in search of jobs. Vast bulk of such migrants belong to the weaker section of society having only their labour power to sell. The city, up to a point, is able to absorb them as cheap labour, but is not built to accommodate them. Their contribution to the city's economy and other services is of paramount importance, but they are relegated to sub-human conditions of living. "A labourer's eight hours of work is useful for 'economic growth and development', but his needs of housing, public transport, water supply and other civic amenities for the remaining sixteen

hours become 'urban problems'." These people, left with no
option, therefore, put up temporary structures, without following any building regulations, on such vacant space in the city
where initially there is no objection or opposition. Such highly
congested shanty structures are often deprived of free air and
light, lack totally in basic amenities and finally emerge as very
unhygienic places unworthy of human existence. Slums are,
thus, the result of structural inequalities in society.

These generalisations are eminently applicable to the cities
of the Third World countries. This does not mean, however,
that the cities of the First World countries did not have slums
or do not have them today. It has become a part of our common
knowledge that almost all big urban agglomerations in U.S.A.
and the European countries had worst kinds of slums in the
past. And in spite of phenomenal generation of wealth and scien-
tific development during the course of modern history since
Industrial Revolution, these countries have not been able to
eradicate ghettos and slums from their big urban industrial
centres.

II

The city of Bombay like other industrial and commercial
centres in the country has passed through the same experience.
As it expanded industrially and commercially so did the number
of its squatter settlements grow and the slums proliferated. In
Bombay, as the records show, squatting began during the inter-
war period but large-scale population influx did not commence
until the 1940s. Large number of migrants who entered the city
during this period continue to live in squatter settlements till
today.

As the city grew from a fishermen's land of seven tiny islands
to a huge industrial-commercial place the squalor of the residential areas of the poor also increased. According to one author,
by the turn of the century the city of Bombay was 'as foul as
some medieval slum.' The 1911 census figures show that sixty-
nine per cent of the population lived in one room dwellings.
According to 1931 census data, on an average 4.4 people lived
together in each of the two lakh fifty thousand tenements. Out
of these two and a half lakh tenements two lakh tenements had

only one room. With the coming of the Second World War and the deepening crisis, there was a very rapid growth of the city's population which in turn aggravated further the housing situation in the city. By 1951 the average occupancy of the living space had risen to 6 persons per room. According to the estimate of 1971 census nearly 77.4 per cent of the households lived in one room units and 14.2 per cent of the households in two-room units. According to a sample survey eightyone per cent of the families living in one room did not have a kitchen. More than two lakh households shared dwellings and nearly one million households lived in hutments and most of them were without basic civic services.

As stated above, Bombay's population has been increasing rapidly since the 1940s. The city had less than a million persons living within its boundary in the beginning of this century. By the end of 1930s this number had risen to nearly 1.69 million. And by the end of 1970s the figure rose to over 8 (eight) million. To be exact as per 1981 census report the city's population was 8.36 million nearly three years ago. The projected population figures for this city are 11.41 million in 1991 and 15.19 million in 2001.

According to one estimate, as mentioned earlier, nearly three hundred (another estimate is of three hundred and fifty) additional hands arrive here every day in search of livelihood. On an average among them there are 25 to 30 families arriving here to settle down permanently. Squatter settlements or 'jhopadpatties' as they are called in the city crop up almost everywhere and all the time in Greater Bombay region as the only answer to the pressing housing needs of these migrants—migrants who are described as 'marginals' to the city and as 'dangerous parasites' by the members of the affluent section of our society. The 'invasion' of squatters in the city is perceived as an assault on private property, and the affluent live in a state of terror as if.

III

Bombay being India's largest industrial and commercial centre, its slums match the vastness and growth of its affluence. These slums unambiguously manifest the extreme polarity of the

city's population. The incapacity of the city's labour force to
have adequate housing finally results in their occupancy of land
preferably near their places of work. Such lands are mostly
uninhabitable—low lying or marshy areas or hilly sites in and
around the city. It is relevant to mention the fact that the government and also the civic authorities did not show much concern
for a long time towards the proliferation of 'illegal' squatter
settlements on public land since the low cost of squatter housing
and the money earned by them through the supply of their cheap
labour to the city's economic and commercial enterprises ensured
that large masses of the poor survive with minimum demands
on the public exchequer. As the subsequent developments have
demonstrated authorities were also able to exercise a kind of
political control over these squatter settlements as there were
several things 'illegal' about their existence in these areas. Under
threat and through manipulation the ruling party was able to
build a political network in these areas and mobilise the votes at
the time of elections. As indicated above, by definition, all
these slums, including those in existence for decades, were (and
are) illegal and liable to be evicted at a moment's notice.

There was a new turn in the slum policy of the State Government in Bombay immediately following independence. It made
an attempt to build 'conventional' houses and to rehouse the
slums dwellers in them. Later, state investments in housing were
deliberately cut and slums allowed to proliferate. This was also
the period when the processes of eviction and demolition of
'undesirable' slums started. It may be of interest to note here
that soon after independence the then Chief Minister of Bombay
Morarji Desai and the Mayor of this city the late S.K. Patil
had a dream and an aspiration to create another 'Paris' out of
this city of Bombay. For the realisation of this dream, the slum
dwellers of Bombay, 'the eyesore of the city, the shanty-ugly
looking spots on the face of the beautiful city' needed to be transferred to the outskirts of the main city. The Municipal Corporation took a decision to work towards the materialization of this
dream. It acquired land at Mankhurd and Jogeshwari (eastern
and northern most areas of the city respectively, about 35 km.
away from the main city limits) and started evicting and trans-
ferring different "jhopadpattis" of Bombay to these places.
When these slums were being demolished and shifted to Man-

khurd in the basin of a hillock on the Sion-Trombay road, the uprooted persons were assured that it was going to be their permanent place of residence. Accordingly, people worked on the land, made it into a habitable one at their own expense and labour. This huge slum colony came to be known as Janata Colony. It emerged almost as a huge bazar and place of residence of nearly 70,000 people. The inhabitants belonging to different faiths and linguistic groups lived here in peace and harmony for nearly 25 years. But to their dismay and horror all their homes were destroyed and demolished with the help of the armed police force on 17th May 1976. We have some details on this colony in the section on case-history.

IV

Eviction was not uncommon in the decade following independence, but it was not as rampant as we find it today. By 1960s very large slums had been established in Bombay and these consolidated themselves over time into "permanent" settlements. The sheer size of these working class colonies coupled with the impossibility of controlling-in-migration meant that these slums had come to stay. The government and the civic authorities continued with their attitude of neglect. Slum improvement programmes were starved of funds mainly out of a fear that if slums are improved they would attract even more migrants. Living conditions in the slums, thus, were allowed to deteriorate.

A recent study on the housing situation of the underprivileged section of the city has made a very apt remark. It says "until recently the place of the city's poor had been largely hidden under the rock of urban profits, especially those of private builders, industrialists and traders. But now it seems this reserve army of cheap labour has really grown and expanded itself well beyond the utilising capacity of the city's employers. Consequently, the city's rulers have become urgently concerned with its urban poor because their wretchedness and destitution can no longer be hidden".[1] They are, therefore, referred to as 'eye sore', they now pose a 'barrier to economic growth' and a 'threat to the social order' and they intensify 'the developing crisis in the legitimacy of the city as a centre of prosperity and profits'.

So the poor unanimously emerge as a burden on the city since
they can no longer be used productively (as a supply of cheap
labour), or always controlled effectively. They now come to
represent 'a major threat to the city's middle and upper classes'
in the form of 'health hazards, increased wage demands, congestion, strikes, morchas and communal riots'.

It is against this background that one can understand the
logic behind the slum eradication (demolition and eviction of
slum colonies) as also the slum relocation, improvement and
resettlement policies of the State Government and the civic authorities in Bombay in particular and other cities of Maharashtra
in general. One of the important features, probably the most
important feature of these policies, has been to create a situation
where large section of the slum colonies become 'illegal' and
thus liable to eviction. A careful analysis of the different Acts
passed by the government and the Boards constituted for housing,
slum improvement etc. during 1960s and 1970s, the slum census
operation of 1976 and the process of eviction set-in during 1950s
would reveal this fact. This has become so apparent now.
Demolition and eviction of the slums rather than their improvement and resettlement have become the major preoccupation
of the civic authorities in Bombay.

V

A brief mention of some of these Boards and their declared
objectives before we present some facts and figures relating to
the existing slums in the city may be useful. A detailed discussion on the relevant Acts relating to the slum relocation and
improvement programmes will follow later in a separate chapter.

Prior to the establishment of the Slum Improvement Board,
1973, slum improvement schemes were being executed by agencies like the Bombay Improvement Trust, the Bombay Development Directorate, the Maharashtra Housing Board, the
Municipal Corporation of Bombay.

These organisations carried out the improvement work with
financial assistance from the Central Government. The Maharashtra Housing Board was given the responsibility of the Slum
Improvement Programme on the state government lands in
Maharashtra, including Greater Bombay. One Officer on special

duty was appointed for this purpose. In the case of the Municipal Corporation of Greater Bombay a new department called the Slum Improvement Cell was formed in 1969 to put into effect the slum improvement work in a better co-ordinated way. This cell was formed and it made ward-wise lists of hutment colonies on Municipal lands and prepared detailed inventories in some of the hutment colonies. It also prepared schemes for providing amenities to the various colonies and to expedite its programme. The cell was put under the charge of an Executive Engineer who prepared the schemes, plans, estimates and executed the works after calling tenders or quotations etc.

However, in course of time the government felt the need to introduce a uniform pattern of slum improvement. For this purpose a coordinating body for slum improvement programmes in Maharashtra called the Slum Improvement Board was constituted in February 1974 for providing more 'effectively' and 'speedily', the amenities to the slum areas.

The Slum Improvement Board is now the principal executive organ of the state government for implementing the programme, to provide basic amenities to the slum dwellers. Some of the major functions of the Board are :

(a) To undertake and carry out such improvement works as it considers necessary in the slum improvement areas.

(b) To undertake the maintenance and repairs of the existing amenities.

(c) To collect service charges recoverable.

(d) To collect compensation in respect of the Government lands included in their slum improvement areas.

(e) To entrust, wherever necessary, the slum improvement work for their maintenance or collection of service charges to the Housing Board, the Improvement Trust etc.

(f) To ensure that slum dwellers are themselves involved in the improvement programmes, provision has been made for nomination by the Board of a panchayat in slum areas.

(g) Board has to effect acquisition of private lands declared as slum improvement areas, at the value of sixty times the average monthly rental.

(h) Board has to control further growth of huts and worsen-
ing of congestion in slum areas.

As indicated earlier the first policy adopted by the government was that of slum clearance, that is eradication of shanty
colonies and rehousing the slum dwellers in permanent structures built on the same site or elsewhere by subsidising the cost
of construction. But this policy in itself was not quite adequate—
the construction work could not keep pace with the increased
demand, the cost of construction too was continuously on the
increase and the type of houses that were being built were beyond
the rent paying capacity of slum dwellers. The outcome of this
scheme was :

(a) Slum lords manipulated the whole show, renting the
houses to others for exhorbitant amount of money;
(b) Houses were built without providing basic amenities
like water and sanitation ;
(c) So used to living in hutments, the slum dwellers found
it difficult to adapt themselves to the new conditions
of living ;
(d) This led a number of them to rent their own houses
to some one else and they themselves moved to some
other slum area quite satisfied with their shanties ;
(e) Though it was envisaged that the houses will be built
at the same site, in most cases people had to shift
and it often happened that these new areas were far
away from their work site and inaccessible by roads or
railways;
(f) The implementation of this programme was dead slow
and it was found that it was impossible to provide slum
dwellers with well-built houses in the proportion in
which the slum population increased on account of
heavy in-migration.

VI

Bombay's land is owned by five different authorities: 1.
Central Government, 2. State Government, 3. Bombay Municipal Corporation, 4. The Housing Board of Maharashtra and

5. Private individuals including Bombay Port Trust. The squatters and slum colonies are spread on the land owned by these five types of authorities. While the correct estimate of the slum pockets and the number of people living in the slums of Bombay is not available, we do have some sources through which the figures can be checked and also estimated.

On January 4, 1976 a census of slums in the city was carried out under the sponsorship of the State Government. It was a single day head counting operation with the help of seven thousand personnel on the job. It was announced that slum pockets would be identified, the huts on them counted and the slum dwellers there numbered. Householders were to be given identification cards for the purposes of proper settlements in future. This was, in effect, a very haphazard census operation where large number of slum dwellers were left out. This fact was noted by a number of articles which appeared in local dailies and other newspapers. In spite of shortcomings and discrepancies this census of 1976 revealed such features of the slums in Bombay which were never on record before. We present below some of these facts and figures in the form of tables.

The following table indicates the approximate number of the slum pockets, the types of land occupied, the number of hutments and the population figures of slum dwellers.

Spread of slums according to the slum census conducted by the State Government in Bombay on January 4, 1976

Sr. No.	Land Owner	Pockets	Hutments	Population
1.	Central Government	120	39,404	1,97,000
2.	State Government	415	89,751	4,48,000
3.	B.M.C.	309	1,18,000	5,07,000
4.	Housing Board	47	58,061	2,62,000
5.	Private individuals (including B.P.T.)	780	3,22,000	14,50,000
	Total	1,671	6,27,216	28,64,000

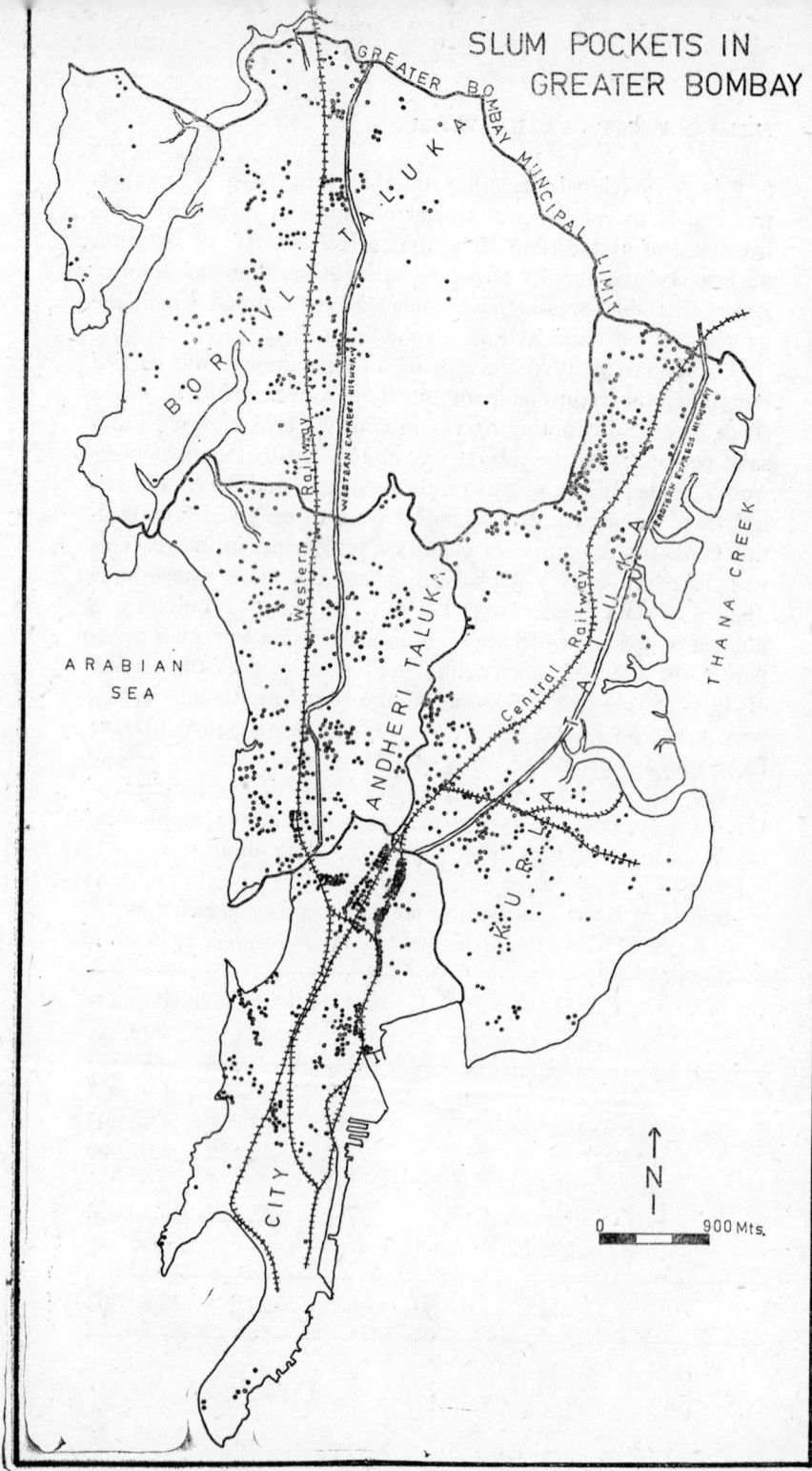

SLUM POCKETS IN GREATER BOMBAY

GREATER BOMBAY MUNICIPAL LIMIT

BORIVLI TALUKA

ANDHERI TALUKA

KURLA TALUKA

CITY

ARABIAN SEA

THANA CREEK

Western Railway

Western Express Highway

Central Railway

Eastern Express Highway

N

0   900 Mts.

According to the details subsequently supplied by "The Times of India", Bombay, the total number of slum pockets were 1,680 and not 1,671 and the number of hutments 6,27,404 and not 6,27,216 as shown in the above table. Again according to the ex-Vice President of MHADA the number of hutments censused in 1976 were 5,87,657 and the total slum population to be 29,57,385 which is much more than the figures specified in the above mentioned census table. Due to this dichotomy there is room to believe that none of the figures related to the hutment colonies population in the city are correct and there are vast number of residents who are neither censused nor any account of them is available with the concerned authorities. During his chief ministership Mr. Sharad Pawar had stated that there were 31 lakhs of slum dwellers in Bombay alone which amounted to almost 50 per cent of the city's population and by now it would be certainly more than this figure.

The following table indicates the per cent distribution of 1976 estimates of total population, employment and slum population according to Municipal Wards in the city of Bombay.

Wardwise per cent distribution of total population and slum population in Greater Bombay (1976)

| Ward | Per Cent Distribution of Population | | |
	Total Population	Slum Population	Employment
A	2.72	0.66	18.62
B	2.57	—	6.02
C	4.48	—	7.17
D	5.78	0.91	5.18
E	7.73	0.91	9.25
F	10.29	7.03	9.89
G	13.17	11.59	17.52
Island City	46.74	21.10	73.65
H	9.34	10.93	2.67
K	10.28	7.94	5.56

L	4.68	10.94	3.69
M	5.79	11.83	2.55
N	8.78	9.76	4.96
Suburbs	38.87	51.40	19.43
P	7.09	7.44	3.56
R	4.98	7.08	2.68
T	2.32	12.98	0.68
Extended Suburbs	14.39	27.50	6.92
Total	100.00	100.00	100.00

It may be observed from the above table that the slum population has been forced to seek shelter relatively away from the
concentration of employment. It may also be seen that the overall
proportion of slum population is 40 per cent, in some parts of
the city it is over 50 per cent.

What are these huts that make a slum colony like? What are
the materials used? Mud, grass, leaves, timber planks, gunny
bags and things like these are ingeniously used by the people in
the slum areas to shelter themselves. We have some figures and
relevant details below.

According to the 1971 census, between 1961 and 1971 mud-
houses in Bombay increased by 300 per cent. Whereas houses
having grass, leaves or timber planks as roofing material have
grown by 250 per cent. The slum census of 1976 brought out
some more features.

The huts have an average area of 133 sq. ft. or 12.5 sq. metres.
They are constructed with the use of unconventional materials
like untreated waste wooden planks, GI sheet panels, gunny
cloth, polythene, bamboo mats etc., for walling as well as for
roofing. Some huts make partial use of conventional building
materials like clay-tile roofs, brickwalls up to a sill height or
IPS flooring etc. Most of these huts are not a finished product
at a point in time but display an incremental process based on
factors like availability of finance, security of tenure, nature of
jobs, etc.

The hut is mostly a single room enclosure though there are huts with more than one room also. In fact a recent phenomenon has been that two-storeyed rickety structures of wood planks are increasing in the suburbs as the densities and family sizes increase.

Most of the huts do not incorporate any sanitary facilities like a bath or W.C. within the hut. In the far-flung sparsely populated village-like slums one does find a tarpaulin or gunny cloth enclosure outside the hut for purpose of bath. The majority do not have independent water taps. All such needs are fulfilled by common services which are generally provided as part of the slum improvement of public authorities. It is a general observation that the slums in the suburbs and extended suburbs have mostly come up on lands which at that time were not suitable for development of conventional shelters, i.e. low-lying marshy lands prone to flooding in monsoons, hill slopes, open spaces next to railway tracks, major roadways, etc.

Slums have also appeared on private lands which may be designated for public purpose in the Development Plan and hence were liable for compulsory acquisition. However, since the compensation payable for such acquisition is far below the real market rate and municipal resources have not been adequate enough to acquire all such lands even at these low rates, the land owners either passively allowed the slums to grow or in some cases promoted them. Now the situation seems to have changed. We will discuss it in some detail later.

Most of the slum dwellers carry out minor repairs and other maintenance jobs to keep the floor and roof together especially so before the monsoons. However, any permanent structural changes are not allowed according to the rules laid down by the Controller of Slums. The rules specially prohibit any changes that would alter the present temporary and *kutcha* nature of the slum-dwellings.

VII

The Slum Census of 1976 enumerated the socio-economic indicators of Bombay slums which are given in the table below.

Selected Socio-Economic Indicators of Slums (1976)

1.	Average size of households	4.38 persons
2.	% of workers to total persons	32.68%
3.	Average number of workers per household	1.47
4.	Average income per month	

(i) per household	..	Rs.	419.00
(ii) per person	..	Rs.	94.00
(iii) per worker	..	Rs.	285.00

5.	Average rent paid per household	Rs. 15.02
6.	Females per thousand males	754
7.	% of household giving rent	47.92%

A recent sample survey conducted in four major slums of Bombay portrays the following features:[2]

Selected Socio-Economic Indicators of Slums
(A Survey done in 1979)

1.	Average size of households	..	4.92 persons
2.	Workers per household—average	..	1.32 persons
3.	Single worker households	..	70%
4.	2 workers households	..	20%
	3 workers per household	..	5%
	No. workers per household	..	3%
5.	Average number of children	..	2.14
6.	Unemployment rate	..	21%
7.	Duration of stay :		
	more than 15 years	..	75%
	less than 15 years	..	25%
8.	Labour-force (above 10 years)	..	33%
	informal sector	..	24%
	formal sector	..	56%
9.	Household income per month		
	Less than Rs. 500	..	66%
	Rs. 501 and above	..	33%

It is observed further that irrespective of formal or informal sector employment the jobs are generally menial or low-skilled indicating low levels of acquired urban skills among the slum dwellers. The result is low incomes. The following income groups form Bombay's slums.

An Income-wise Distribution of Slum Households
Slum Census (1976)

Sr. No.	Monthly income group (Rs.)	Percentage of slum households
1.	Less than 200	12.12
2.	200—350	28.01
3.	350—600	38.58
4.	600—1000	14.14
5.	1000 and above	3.86
6.	Not recorded	3.29

It may be seen from the above table that 79 per cent of slum households belong to low income groups with monthly incomes below Rs. 600/-. Median monthly income per household is Rs. 400/-. Another feature which the above table brings out, and is relevant for public policy, is that 40 per cent of slum households fall in EWS category and another 39 per cent in IIG category.

Further studies on the unorganized or informal sector which forms a major part of slums' labour force indicate that not only are the incomes in this sector lower than that of the formal sector but that they also tend to stabilize at low levels and remain stagnant thereafter. Some studies of slums indicate that such phenomenon is observed for employees in the formal sector as well. In one such study it is observed that the average earning of a wage employee in the age group of 20-24 years is Rs. 267/- which stabilises at Rs. 350/- at the age of 30-34.

The stagnating income also inhibits the mobility of the slum dwellers. It has been observed in a number of studies that the majority of slum dwellers have stayed in the slums for over 15 years. The common notion that shelter is sought in slums by new migrants as a transient accommodation is thus not true in the case of Bombay.

NOTES

1. Colin Gonsalves, *op. cit.* (see Foreword).
2. This Sample survey was conducted by the Maharashtra Housing and Area Development Authority (MHADA), see "Non-conventional And Alternative Approaches to Shelter. The Urban Poor : Experience in Bombay" (Mimeographed), Seminar Secretariate C/o MHADA, Griha Nirman Bhawan, Bandra (E), Bombay-51.

CHAPTER TWO

THE SLUM PROBLEM AND THE PLANNING PROCESS

I

In the preceding chapter we presented a picture of the growth and proliferation of slums in Bombay. As indicated in the introduction there is a close relationship between slum proliferation and city planning. Urban planning in general and housing programmes in particular are always marked by an ideology which determines the course of urban development. Experience has shown that our urban planning has not only been lopsided and without a vision to foresee the future needs of the towns and the cities in general, it has also been highly discriminatory to the poor in terms of making provisions for their accommodation facilities and the basic services needed for their everyday existence. The town planning process in Maharashtra can be looked at as a case in point. We quote here at same length a recent study which examines this process with particular reference to Bombay and Pune historically in some details :

The first Town Planning Act was passed in 1915. It enabled local authorities to prepare Town Planning Schemes for open areas within their jurisdictions which were in the process of development (being built). This Act which was based on the British Town Planning Act of 1909 introduced a model of urban form "characterised by low-density, low rise development which was quite contrary to the previous urban tradition determined by indigenous family structure,

17

the urban economy prevailing technology as well as cultured institutions" (King, 1976). Indigenous towns had grown without any formal plans. They were compact with buildings close to each other along narrow alleyways, as no motorised transport was available; residences, craft industry, storage facilities were not laid out in separate areas but were intermingled. Such features of old towns were now regarded as undesirable. 'Modern' town planning saw the future development quite distinct from the traditional urban form, with separation of various activities, uncongested development with open spaces around buildings, wide roads and amplitude of basic services. The Town Planning Act was introduced in order to plan new development in a formal manner to avoid haphazard and unregulated extension of towns and to ensure orderly development.

The Act laid down an elaborate procedure for 'reconstituting' original, in most cases agricultural, landholdings into regular building plots, with land reserved for public purposes, roads etc. and for calculating the amount of 'net demand' by the local authority. The cost of the scheme was to be met partly or totally from contributions levied by the local authority on each 'final' plot in the scheme. They were calculated on the basis of the increment which was estimated to accrue to each owner due to the proposed development of the area. The whole procedure was cumbersome, time consuming and complicated.

In 1954, this Act was superseded by a new Town Planning Act. It made it obligatory on local authorities to prepare development plans for the whole of the area within their jurisdiction. The objective was to plan for comprehensive development of a city rather than planning for parts of it. Preparing individual Town Planning Schemes for different areas of the city was seen as leading to unco-ordinated and disaggregated development without adequate linkages between individual 'planned' areas. The preparation, therefore, of an overall plan for the city was regarded as a precondition to ensure its orderly and regulated growth. This Act brought the whole of the area of a city under formal planning and town planning schemes (as specified in the Act 1915) were now required to be prepared within the framework of a city development plan. Even built up areas could now be included in town planning schemes.

A development plan is primarily a land-use map. It contains proposals for zoning the development in various residential, commercial, and industrial areas, allocations of land for public purposes such as open spaces, hospitals, schools, infrastructural development such as roads, sewerage, drainage, water and electricity etc., traffic and transportation. The document is accompanied by information regarding the cost of land acquisition, estimates of works, phases of development. Development control rules regulate the division of larger landholdings into individual building plots and Floor Space Index (maximum allowable built up area in relation to the area of the plot). Building bye-laws specify the standards of structural quality and area of accommodation to be provided.

A dominant school of thought regarding 'minimum standards' which is still persistent is well illustrated by the following extract from an editorial in the Journal of the Institute of Town Planners, India (1955) : "The basic standards in housing and planning are arrived at not only from considerations of creating a desirable sociological and physical environment necessary for the healthy growth of the individuals and the community. Such standards have been established by various committees and technical missions. . . recommending a two-roomed house with adequate sanitary facilities as the barest minimum if the normal aspirations of healthy living is to be achieved. . . These standards cannot be lowered, whatever the community, whatever the location and whatever the economic situation in the country. Substandard housing is but a step towards slums. Deliberate sub-standard housing will lead towards the creation of future slums. The basic standards must be adhered to at all costs."

The Maharashtra Regional and Town Planning Act was passed in 1966. This Act enlarged the scope of planning further to include the region surrounding metropolitan and industrial centres. The earlier Act had provided for the preparation of city development plans. But there was considerable, mainly industrial, development just outside the city

limits of some of the industrial centres. The new Act, therefore, was an attempt to ensure adequate infrastructural development and orderly growth in the region surrounding an
industrial centre. It also made possible development of new
towns in such regions if it was 'expedient in the public
interest' to do so.

The Regional Plan is also a land-use map. It shows
allocation of land for various purposes—residential, industrial, agricultural, forests, mining, reservation of areas as
nature reserves, for dairies, animal sanctuaries, etc. It contains proposals for the network of transport and communi-
cation, conservation and development of natural resources
and "such other matters as are likely to have an important
influence on the development of the region".

Whatever the eloquence of the exposition in the regional
plans they remain largely paper documents because of the
lack of funds to carry out the development envisaged in the
plans and also owing to the absence of a metropolitan wide
coordinating and implementing agency, except for the Bombay
Metropolitan Regional Development Authority though, even
there, fears persist that the BMRDA might just be another
tier—"just a net over the tossed salad and not a dressing to
garnish it" (Sivaramkrishnan, 1975-76).

City development plans which are to be implemented
by the local administration also remain declarations of pious
intentions. Both finance for, and management of, urban
development at the local level remain major stumbling blocks.
Without these statutory requirements of providing estimates
of works and statement of cost and phases of development as
part of the plan document, such plans remain mere academic
exercises. Such problems would remain "unless the financing,
planning and management of urban development is co-
ordinated such that local authorities can be held responsible"
(Mohan, 1982).

With each successive piece of legislation, the area under
physical planning has been enlarged. Each successive Act
contains within it provisions of the earlier Act with only
minor modifications, if any. Passing of each new Act does
not seem to have involved a critical appraisal of the tenets

on which Town Planning has been based: idealistic planning norms which are at variance with the socio-economic context continue to be insisted upon. In fact, planning hardly relates to the complexities of modern economic life.

Town planning regards as its central problem the distribution of the population within a given territory. It stresses the need for controlling population density per acre to ensure hygienic and pleasant environment. It assumes, for example, that the problems of congestion and housing occur because too many people live or work in a certain area. This diagnosis has resulted in developing an obsession among town planners with controlling the number of people living in a particular locality and an equally powerful obsession with stopping in-migration. Another manifestation of this obsession is the introduction around cities of 'green belts' to prevent urban sprawl. Its paradoxical consequence is reproduction of urban sprawl beyond an urban area and consequent problems of increased transportation and commuter costs (Harris, 1982).

On the question of housing it is assumed that private building activity will cater to the housing needs of a large majority of the city residents. As a welfare measure those who are too poor to afford even rented accommodation are supposed to be given subsidised public housing. Such categories include what are euphemistically called Economically Weaker Section (EWS, monthly income below Rs. 350) and Low Income Group (LIG, monthly income between Rs. 351 to Rs. 600).

Experience so far shows that with escalation of land prices and costs of construction, an increasingly larger proportion of the urban population has found it impossible to compete in the urban housing market. The problem is made more acute by the insistence on minimum plot sizes and standards of construction and accommodation. At the same time, government has been able to build only very few subsidised housing units to accommodate a negligible proportion of the needy households. A former Director of Housing and Urban Development Corporation (HUDCO) is scathing regarding the present approach to housing. "We delude

ourselves into thinking that we are giving people better housing by attaching a subsidy to the few houses we build for the
EWS..A subsidy has to be very heavy to bring a Rs. 10,000
house within reach of an EWS family. Apart from this, a
subsidy policy limits the size of a housing programme very
heavily, because it depends closely on year to year budgetary
constraints. Also, a heavy subsidy inevitably leads to dispos-
session of the poor and deserving by people who are better-
off and are able to buy out the original allottees by resorting
to subterfuges like sub-letting; the poor people are then
back in their hovels" (D'Souza, 1975). This phenomenon
of the poor renting out their subsidised tenements and moving
out into hutments is not understood as a process of dis-
possession; it is generally interpreted as a manifestation of
their 'slum mentality' which implies that they 'prefer' to live
in squalid and wretched conditions. In reality, however,
given the situation of acute scarcity of housing even for the
middle income group, it must be seen as an expression of
their economic rationality to trade their housing for cash to
supplement their less than subsistence level incomes.

The present approach to town planning and housing, in
the absence of determined steps to control land prices is
a recipe for increasing polarisation in living conditions of the
rich and the poor. In the name of creating an orderly, hygienic and aesthetically pleasing environment, it in fact denies
the poor access to adequate housing and environment. It
is discriminatory for it creates 'planned' development at the
cost of the availability of even basic services to the poor;
they are forced to become illegal, unauthorised city residents
because they do not have the means to afford even 'minimum'
authorised accommodation.[1]

II

It is in this context, the fact of the inability on the part of
the government and lack of political will that one has to examine
the recent development in the area of so-called measures like
relocation and improvements of slums in Bombay. Municipal

Corporation of Greater Bombay adopted the measures for the clearance of the areas "unfit for human habitation" and "dangerous or injurious" to the health of the inhabitants thereby making a provision in the Bombay Municipal Corporation Act under section 354 (R) as early as 1954. The purpose of this measure was a systematic eradication of the areas identified as slums—areas considered as a place where "undesirable" people live and often live a life as a "lawless citizen". A separate ministry of housing came into existence to look into this problem and prepare ground for action.

During the first decade after independence the government adopted the policy of the slum clearance, i.e., eradication of shanty colonies and rehousing the slum dwellers in permanent structures built on the same site or elsewhere by subsidising the cost of construction. The work of construction could not keep pace with ever increasing housing demands. The cost of construction kept on increasing and the type of houses built were beyond the rent-paying capacity of the slum dwellers. Proper maintenance of the buildings and inalienability of the premises could not be ensured. The outcome of this scheme was, as pointed out earlier, the following :

(a) Houses were built without providing basic amenities like water and sanitation.

(b) Slum lords manipulated the whole show by renting the houses to others and expropriating exhorbitant amount of money.

(c) Though it was envisaged that the houses will be built at the same site, in most cases slum dwellers were forced to shift and it happened generally that these new areas were far away from their work site and inaccessible by roads or railways.

(d) slum-dwellers, in several cases, traded their houses for cash and went away to settle elsewhere quite satisfied, as if, with their old shanties.

This thoughtless and callous implementation of the slum clearance programme did not succeed in eradicating the slums. They kept on cropping up on new sites and thus proliferating.

It was, therefore, thought that there should be a programme for improving the basic amenities in the existing slums so that the dwellers there have better conditions of living.

The slum improvement cell of the Municipal Corporation of Greater Bombay was formed in 1969 along with the Housing Board (The Slum Improvement Board). This Board became responsible to carry out the improvement work with financial assistance from the Central Government. The Policy was to improve existing slums by providing essential civic amenities like water, approach road, street light, drainage, latrines etc.

This programme of improvement covered the types of slums situated on the state government's land and on the land of Municipal Corporation where the basic amenities did not exist. The Slum Improvement Board did not take up the functional responsibility of the programme. It assigned the responsibility to some other agencies like the Municipal Corporation etc.

Another measure adopted in the seventies was to demolish the slums and shift them to the outskirts of the city on open plots of land preserved for the resettlement of thus evicted slums. As a blind adoption of such a policy was likely to result in severe dislocation of the economic life and the general living condition* of the hutment dwellers in particular and also the city in general, the government of Maharashtra decided to tackle this problem on humanitarian grounds and on a high priority basis. This was known as Environmental Improvement Scheme where the governmental resolution clearly specified that the Act of slum demolition will be implemented with due caution and restraint and that no slum will be demolished and cleared in a manner that the residents thereof are thrown away to remote parts of the city. It was also envisaged that the success of demolition and resettlement programme would ultimately depend on the active support and participation of the slum dwellers themselves. As is well known these objectives remained on paper only and there were several cases of demolition and eradication of slums with the use of physical force and without any humanitarian consideration.

---

*And this is what exactly happened. We have some newspaper reports included in this report to show their miserable plight.

III

The slum dwellers' residences, another name for squalor and filth, have attracted the attention of some voluntary agencies and they too have played some role in slum improvements in Bombay which need recognition. These agencies have acted sometimes as intermediary between the government and the slum-dwellers. The problem of slums in Bombay is vitally linked with the city administration. Any voluntary agency naturally cannot do much without the sanction and/or the support o the government and the city administration. Lions and Rotary clubs are two such agencies which claim to have come forward to do this social work. Their efforts can best be described as a patch-work helping selected slums in improving the conditions of living thereby providing some civic amenities. As pointed out such improvements have ended up at best as marginal solution of the problem of the problem. A strike at the root has been far from the sight.

The Reserve Bank of India came out with a proposal to finance housing for the poor through the services of the nationalised Banks in the country. The Government of Maharashtra came forward to make use of this provision by asking for a soft loan of rupees fifteen crores for the urban housing scheme for the poor and the slum dwellers in the city ot Bombay. In this scheme of housing for the urban poor the government proposed to pay special attention to the members of the scheduled castes and the scheduled tribes. The policy was based on the view that there will be an attempt to mobilise the resources out of the saving of the economically weaker section of the community and they will be motivated to invest as much as they can in constructing a house and own it. As far as this programme is concerned it has remained more as a pious intention rather than an actively pursued and followed-upon action. A few houses were built of course, in a particular course of time, but these also went to the people who did not originally belong to the slums and for whom they were not built. It should also be mentioned here that several such houses ended up as substandard construction with cracks in the walls and leaking roofs and naturally unoccupied in several cases. Who was going to invest his hard earned money in such houses?

In the next chapter we will have a look at the housing question and the vacant land in the context of slums in the city.

NOTE

1. Meera Bapat, "Hutments and City Planning", Economic and Political Weekly, March 12, 1983.

CHAPTER THREE

THE HOUSING QUESTION AND
THE VACANT LAND

I

Greater Bombay and its neighbouring urban areas have been growing at about 4 per cent per annum for the last couple of decades. However, the concomitant improvement required in urban infrastructure particularly in housing, as pointed out earlier, has not kept pace with the population growth. As against the annual need of 60,000 housing units the supply of 'formal' housing units has been around 15,000 to 20,000 in recent past. The large proportion of population staying in slums, about 40 per cent in 1976 and more than (approximately) 50 per cent as of now, is a manifestation not only of this gap between the need and the supply in the formal sector but also of the total unconcern and lack of consideration for 'equity' in the provision of public housing. The population seeking shelter outside the formal housing supply has been growing at a rate faster than that of the overall population. Bombay which had a population of 0.8 million at the beginning of the century is likely to have around 15 million people by the turn of this century. The present population of the City is more than 8.36 million (1981 census).

The estimated annual housing need is around 60,000 units with a household size of 5. According to one estimate the annual need of housing of Greater Bombay has followed and is likely to follow the following pattern:[1]

27

Period	Incremental Population (Million)			Annual Housing Need
1961—71	...	1.82	...	40,000
1971—81	...	2.39	...	50,000
1981—91	...	3.05	...	60,000
1991—2001	...	3.78	...	80,000

In terms of formulating any forward-looking and even seemingly progressive policy towards meeting the housing needs of the less 'fortunate' and the poorer sections in the city, the performance of the State Government has been dismal. As the records show the Government has increasingly tilted its policy towards the builders, speculators and the owners of large tracts of land in the City. This becomes clear when one looks at the fate the famous Urban Land (Ceiling and Regulation) Act of 1976 has met in the City. What follows in the second section of this chapter, is an account of the performance of the State Government in terms of the implementation of the above noted Act. Before we present this account we would like to quote here a portion of a letter written sometime back by the members of the Association of Practising Architects in Bombay to the central and the State Governments after they failed to get an appointment with the authorities to appraise them of the crisis on housing front in the City. It reads as follows: "As professionals we have welcomed the basic idea behind the Urban Land (Ceiling and Regulation) Act 1976. At the same time we will be failing in our duty if we do not record that the Act as it exists (and the manner of implementation particularly by the Government of Maharashtra) is doing more harm than good. The operation of the Act has resulted in skyrocketing prices of residential accommodation, chaotic condition in the field of housing, tremendous increase in the spurt of illegal structures and great increase in corruption in city areas, placing even the smallest accommodation beyond the reach of common man. But more than this, the apathy of Maharashtra Government is intriguing".

So far pleas by all sections of Society, fears and frustrations expressed particularly by the middle and lower income groups (the very poor are incapable of even making any demand) have fallen on deaf ears.

The new flats are purchased by the speculators. In recent past the failure of Special Bearer Bonds Scheme created a fear that the Government would find other ways of unearthing cash. Thus, people with black money invested it in flats. Builders themselves hold between 15 per cent to 20 per cent of their unsold flats at any given time. The ownership flat market is in fact in the hands of speculators who have now made even Bombay's suburbs beyond the reach of people belonging to the middle classes and the lower middle classes. As a result the housing situation has become extremely critical.

II

The question of urban housing is inextricably linked with the availability of land in an urban area. The fate of the urban poor in terms of his day-to-day living in a city is, therefore, directly linked with the availability of vacant land for building such low cost houses which the economically poor section of the urban community can afford. Acquisition of such land by the Government in all the cities of the country has become an unsurmountable problem because of the vested interests in urban land. The Planning Commission seemed to realise this fact at a stage and outlined the specific problems of urban growth as:[2]

1. Excessive and speculative rise in urban land values ;
2. The pocketing of the gains from appreciation of land values resulting from public investment, by private owners of land ;
3. The unequal distribution of urban land among different classes of society; buildings and regulations conducive to exclusive and sub-optional use of developed land by the elite minorities ;
4. As a result of highly unequal income distribution, limited savings, large scale indebtedness of the vast masses, and the need to spend over 60 per cent of income on food by the lower and working classes, these sections are unable to finance the minimum development cost of land ;

> 5. Lastly, the large scale concentration of land owner-
>   ship in the hands of a few.

The Planning Commission came out with such an analysis in 1974 and defined its urban land policy accordingly. Promotion of an optimum use of land, making land available for purposes of economic growth consistent with social justice, particularly to the economically weaker sections of society, reducing and preventing, if possible, concentration of land ownership, rising land values, and speculation, and finally using land as a resource for financing urban development were the main contents of its draft Fifth Five-Year Plan 1974, vol. II.

This was followed by the famous 44th Constitution Amendment which brought into existence the Urban Land (Ceiling and Regulation) Act passed in 1976. This Amendment diluted the validity of the right to private property as a fundamental right. The main aim of the Urban Land (Ceiling and Regulation) Act was stated as "preventing the concentration of urban land in the hands of a few persons, and speculation and profiteering therein, with a view to bringing about an equitable distribution of land in urban agglomerations to subserve the common good".

This Act has failed to achieve its main aim all over the country wherever the Act was applicable. "The implementation of the Act has experienced great difficulties and the State Governments have not been able to implement it effectively. There is a general feeling that costs of land have increased substantially both of private land as well as of land owned by public agencies. As a result fears are expressed that urban housing might become too expensive for a large number of people..there have been enormous and unwarranted increases in land values..." (Government of India: *Sixth Five-Year Plan*, 1980-85). Further, to quote another official source in Maharashtra, "It may be seen that the price for a 30 sq. mtrs. flat would be around Rs. 28,000. Since most of these proposals are outright sale of flats without much assistance from institutional finance, it is obvious that such schemes do not reach the poor and largely serve the middle and higher income groups. Moreover at present on account of larger number of litigations that are involved for acquisition of such land, *the Act is being implemented more through its provisions about exemptions and less through its main provisions.* Thus the objectives of the legislation have remained only on the statute books and a major opportunity to have land policies condutive to the solution of problems of shelter for the poor seems t o have been lost" (Emphasis ours) (Seminar Secretariat, MHADA, Theme Papers submitte d to the Seminar on: Non-Conventional and Alternative App roaches to Shelter, the Urban Poor : Experience in Bombay, page 31).

The above note d observation is corroborated by a number of reports pr epared by concerned scholars and journalists on the performance of the State Government in Maharashtra in relation to the implementation of this Act in the city of Bombay. Some of these reports present exhaustive and detailed account of the land vacant in the city and its suburbs which can be utilized for building low cost houses and making provisions for the accommodation of the poor in the city. These reports also show clearly that the main provisions of the UL (C & R) Act have been violated by the office of the State Government itself through various ways of circumvention and manipulation of the Act in favour of the land owners, builders, real estate speculators and the rich in the city. We reproduce below these details brought out by the above-mentioned reports during the course of last three years. For reproduction of these facts we have largely depended on an excellent essay entitled "Requiem For An Act",[3] published in a booklet form. Facts and figures have also been drawn from reports and write-ups published in the local newspapers during the above-mentioned period. We begin with the account of the land vacant in the city and their owners.

Some of the major owners of vast stretches of vacant land in Bombay are charitable trusts. The most noteworthy among them are those of the Wadia Trust at Kurla, F.E. Dinshaw at Mulund, Soli Godrej at Vikroli, Byramji Jeejeebhoy at Goregaon, the C.B. Sharma purchase of the former Yusuf Khot at Kanjur and Powai, the N.D. Sawant Khot at Borivli and Ekhar, the Surai Ballabhdas holdings at Hariyali and the N.I. Mehta holdings at Bhandup.

Three thousand two hundred hectares of unencroached and unencumbered urban land comprise the Godrej holding at Vikhroli. Out of this 200 hectares though "empty" in the conventional sense is classified by the Government as non-vacant under section 2(q) and, therefore, reserved as a private park.

Of the F.E. Dinshaw lands at Malad and Goregaon about 160 hectares though unutilised, falls within (2q) definition of non-vacant, which is therefore to be retained by the landowner. Nusli Wadia of Bombay Dyeing and Ram Batra are both members of the F.E. Dinshaw Trust.

Under Section 20 of the UL (C & R) Act exemptions are granted for public housing. What constitutes "public housing"? According to an Urban Development Department circular to the BMC (No. TPB-4379/UD-5) of 7.1.1980, even co-operative societies qualify as "public housing" irrespective of the class of people who form the society.

Under Section 22 of the same Act exemptions are freely granted. In late 1979 Abdul Majid Abdulla Patel, better known as Yusuf Patel, a former COFEPOSA detenu, asked for, and was granted, exemption (number 1527) under Section 22 of the Act, to redevelop a plot, despite the fact that a building on the site was under contract of repair to the Bombay Repairs and Reconstruction Board of the MHADA, since the tenants had paid a cess to the Board. The executive engineer who visited the site found the demolition under way and wrote to Patel asking him why this was being done without a certificate from the Board. Under Section 91(5) of the MHADA Act a prior NOC (No Objection Certificate) of the Board is obligatory. Patel was silent and instead finished knocking the building down.

In February 1981, however, Yusuf Patel's disregard for the Board's NOC's proved to be an intelligent act, for the housing department waived the Board's NOC. Yusuf Patel then went on to build luxury flats and a shopping centre at Nagpada in Bombay.

This is only part of the story. In March 1980, UL (C & R) permission (number 1563) under Section 22 was granted to Haji S. Asgar Ali (C/o. architect B. K. Gupta) and a 20-storey building "Sabu Baug" was constructed next to Anjuman-i-Islam High School. The three block "Bustaan Apartments", also on this road, was granted UL (C & R) clearance (number 1272) on 12.7.1979 in the name of Usman Ibrahim Batwa, although the building was developed jointly by Yusuf Patel and Haji Mastaan (another noted COFEPOSA detenu).

Further down the road is A.M. Potia Apartments given UL (C & R) NOC (number 14622) on 23.11.1979. The pattern is repeated over and over again. Under Section 21(1) of the Act the State Government grants exemptions for those vacant land owners who propose to use the land for building dwellings for the E.W.S. Half the buildable area so exempted is to be used for tenements not exceeding 40 m^2. Those who obtain such exemption must begin construction within one year of the exemption order and complete the construction within five years. The selling price is set at a maximum of Rs. 90 per ft^2 for E.W.S. This has now been increased.

Now the time period within which construction is to begin and completed is not always complied to since the Government has no machinery (or no intention) to follow up the exemption order. Owners of excess vacant land may, therefore, leave their exempted plots unbuilt hoping for a change in the Government and/or the Act itself, sometime in the future.

Even if houses are built there is no guarantee that they will go to the poor. Firstly the price stipulated for sale (Rs. 90 per ft^2) is a nominal one because the Government has no machinery for supervising sales. The actual rates are as high as five times the stipulated rate, many of the transactions going on in "black".

Secondly, the Government nowhere insists that the houses built for the E.W.S. actually be bought by them because it has no mechanism to check whether the buyers are actually members of the E.W.S. with a family income less than Rs. 350 per month. The Government only specifies the size of the unit and the selling price and assumes that only members of the E.W.S. will buy them. In actual fact any person who has money can buy such a tenement.

The smallest tenement for the E.W.S. is 40 m^2 or approximately 400 ft^2. At today's market rates the cost of such a tenement is at least Rs. 1 lakh. As compared to this, the amount a family earning Rs. 250 per month can afford for a house, is approximately Rs. 5,000. The National Sample Survey has indicated that 75 per cent of the urban population have incomes less than Rs. 350 per month and 90 per cent less than Rs. 600 per month.

Another way of circumventing the Act is to officially charge close to the stipulated rate per ft^2 for E.W.S. housing, and to increase the total cost of the flat by charging for "amenities" at grossly exaggerated costs. These amenities are sometimes not

provided at all. This is the common practice of many builders
in the "Four Bungalows" area of Andheri, Bombay.

Further manipulation of the UL (C & R) Act is carried out
by building flats in such a manner that by breaking down a
minor wall, adjacent units of 40 m² can be joined together into
an apartment with an effective built up area of 80 m².

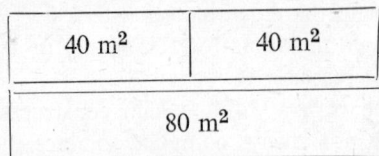

40 m²	40 m²
80 m²	

These will then become satisfactory for the requirements of
the upper income groups who can afford to buy two adjacent
flats in different family members' names.

The Byramjee Jeejeebhoy lands have several major clearances
by Government pending under the Act, for an area totalling 70
hectares. The first is for "weaker section housing" in Oshivara.
The builder is Ajmera.

Another way of circumventing the provisions of the UL
(C & R) Act is by constructing units on the vacant land after
the Act came into force and then backdating the date of construction to escape the Act. There are many such examples of exemptions under Section 2(q).

The Todiwalla lands at Versova have an exemption granted
for five hectares to build 1,200 "weaker section" flats. The T.R.
Patil lands at Mulund have had 6.8 hectares exempted to build
1,100 "weaker section" flats. Some other "weaker section housing" would include Ajmera developed "Yoginagar" at Eskar,
Bafra developed "Veenanagar" on Kertikat owned lands at
Mulund, and Conwood Construction's "Gokulram Yeshwan-
than" on Karmarkar owned lands north of Aarey. These are
just few of the thousands of cases.

Ten per cent of all flats built for E.W.S. are reserved for no-
minees of Government. These flats have been allotted in an entirely discretionary fashion, to journalists and well-known politicians. When contacted, officials of the "Competent Authority"
and the housing department, refused to disclose the list of persons allotted these flats or the basis on which the allotment is
taking place.

The most striking instance is "Raujul" building on Harkness Road with 2-bedroom luxury flats constructed under the weaker section exemption, where the State Government recently offered A.R. Antulay, ex-C.M. of Maharashtra a flat from its 10 per cent Government nominee quota.

Near Andheri, a plot of land existed which was above the ceiling. The moment the Act came into force, the owner put up two unauthorised structures—a gymkhana and another hutment. By bribing the appropriate authorities (usually the talati or city survey officer) he had them registered as "authorised" unauthorised structures and had the receipts backdated to before the Act was passed. The two structures had been in a manner that, if they remained standing, no other permanent building could be built, according to the development rules. The plot was exempted. Today the same plot of land is being used for a high-rise co-operative society.

Most of these manipulations are done with the help of government authorities who maintain land records. Recently a talati of the Santa Cruz office was sacked for backdating records and accepting bribes from owners, builders and contractors.

The UL (C & R) Act is often by-passed by getting permission from the municipality to build, at the same time as an application for exemption is filed with the "Competent Authority". The BMC assuming that the exemption will be granted, allows the building to come up. This, in turn, strengthens the case for exemption, and even if the exemption is not given, acquiring land which has already been built upon is difficult for the Government.

Builders and developers have been unanimous in their opposition to the Act. Ram Dadlani, President, Estate Agents Association of India, complained that the scheme of providing tenements to the E.W.S. is a fraud. "No builder in the city observed the conditions of selling the flats at the rate fixed by the Government. It is not possible for any builder to sell flats at Government rates since the prices of building materials has shot up several times". Therefore, according to him, the Government should allow the market forces to work freely and it was only in this way that a rational pricing system could be reached. Satyamurty, Secretary of the Association of Construction Industries of Maharashtra, said that where there was unlimited demand for construction, the way out was to allow unlimited dwellings to come up. "Any rule or Act which controls construction in terms of size or in any other way is only contributory to the shortage and price hike". Therefore, the UL (C & R) Act, according to him, must be withdrawn.

Contrary to the generally accepted feeling that there is very little land in Bombay, very large areas of buildable land is today lying vacant for one reason or another. There is enough land in Bombay to house the maximum projected population of 15 million by the year 2000 with an F.S.I. of 1 (a very low population density). This land is in the hands of the Government, and is likely to be lost due to the exemption clauses....

It is quite obvious that the formulation of clause 20(1) is extremely vague and hence open to manipulation. Quite a few land holdings have been exempted under section 20 on the grounds that the land was being used for aesthetic purposes.

There are 1,890 cases pending under Section 21(1) of the Act, seeking exemption for a total area of 2,952.83 hectares. The details of the holdings are as follows :

Excess vacant land	No. of cases	Total vacant land (hectares)
1. Up to 10,000 sq. m.	1,599	828.66
2. 10,000 to 15,000 sq. m.	97	124.95
3. 15,000 to 30,000 sq. m.	103	252.89
4. 30,000 to 50,000 sq. m.	22	168.80
5. 50,000 sq. m. and above	69	1477.53

Source : Report of the High Power Steering Group for Slums and Dilapidated Houses, 1981, page 58, table 4.10.

Thus a substantial amount of the total surplus vacant land available in Bombay is lost due to the provisions of Section 21(1).

Let us see how many people can be accommodated if this land was not exempted but used for housing the poor. According to the Development Control (D.C.) Rules about 100 tenements/acre are allowed to be constructed. Assume five persons per tenement on an average and that 3,000 hectares=7,000 acres.

Then the number of people who can be accommodated on land available under Section 21(1)=

$$7,000 \text{ acres} \times 100 \text{ (tenements/acre)}$$
$$\times \quad 5 \text{ (persons per tenement)}$$
$$= \quad 3\tfrac{1}{2} \text{ million.}$$

Thus the entire slum and pavement dweller population of the city can be accommodated simply on the land available under Section 21(1).

These slum dwellers are 50 per cent of the city's population but only occupy 2 per cent of the total land and 12 per cent of the total residential land.

As far as Section 22 is concerned 501 hectares have already been exempted. Besides there are 197 cases involving 400 hectares pending clearance under this section.

Besides these cases, several land holdings have been exempted because they are only marginally in excess of the ceiling limit. However, the extent of this "marginally" excess land are, in some cases, as high as 385 m². MHADA has objected to such exemptions.

Land holdings in industrial zones are exempted by the Directorate of Industries who has special powers of exemption for industrial expansion. Using these special powers approximately 30,000 m² of land in Poisar, in which MHADA was interested was exempted by Directorate of Industries. Likewise many comparatively smaller holdings of approximately 4,000 m² each were exempted for industrial expansion. Exact figures, however, of land area already exempted for industries under this section are not made available to the public.

For any one familiar with the situation in Bombay, it would not take long to realise that the conditions for granting exemptions are likely to lead to a total defeat of the stated objectives of the Act. The State Government is likely to lose all surplus vacant land to the private sector except for some marshy peripheral land. Besides, loss of land through indiscriminate exemptions is bound to affect the resource base of the BMRDA whose aim is to use land as a resource for financing urban development. Thus both from the point of view of making land available to the poorer sections of society and using land as a source of raising finance, the UL (C & R) Act has already developed serious limitations.

III

In March, 1981 the State Government in Maharashtra set up a High Power Steering Group for Slums and Dilapidated Houses (HPSG) under the chairmanship of Ajit Kerkar, Director, Tata Industries, 'to consider the problem of Slums in Greater Bombay and of Dilapidated Houses in the Bombay Island and make concrete recommendations calculated to solve the problem'. In addition to it, the Steering Group was invited to also consider 'appropriate scheme of rehabilitation of entitled slum dwellers' and 'availability of land including surplus land under the Urban Land (Ceiling and Regulation) Act, along with some other matters. The Steering Group submitted its report containing various recommendations in August 1981.

A careful analysis of this report would reveal that the Steering Group, in effect, recommended further dilution of the UL (C & R) Act.[4] For applications pending under Section 21(1) of the Act dealing with the excess land and the ceiling on such land, the Steering Group recommended the table below :

Where the excess vacant land is	No. of cases	To be handed over to Govt. free of charge, value of which to be deposited with Govt.	Further at pre-determined prices	Land to be given to Govt. free of charge
1. Up to 10,000 sq. m.	1,599	15%	15%	Nil
2. 10,000 to 15,000 sq. m.	97	15%	15%	25% above 10,000 sq. m. subject to a minimum of 500 sq. m.

3. 15,000 to 30,000 sq. m.	103	15%	15%	—1250 sq. m. + 30% of land above 15,000 sq. m.
4. 30,000 to 50,000 sq. m.		25%	15%	5750 sq. m. + 35% of land above 30,000 sq. m.
5. 50,000 sq. m. and above	69	15%	15%	12,750 sq. m. + 50% of land above 50,000 sq. m.

Source : Report of the High Power Steering Group for Slums and Dilapidated Houses, 1981, page 58, table 4.10.

This meant that the ceiling was now raised from 500 m^2 to 10,000 m^2, thereby reducing the available surplus vacant land from 2952.83 hectares to 751.25 hectares. The implementation of this recommendation would involve a loss of 2201.58 hectares. Converted into available built-up area this would mean a loss of 160,000,000 ft.^{2}

Regarding the cases pending under Section 20, the HPSG recommended that small pockets be exempted and large holdings be treated on par with Section 21(1). Since it is not likely that there are many holdings larger than 10,000 m^2, the recommendation amounts to a blanket exemption.

Regarding applications pending under Section 22 of the Act, the HPSG recommended that, cases being few, clearances should be liberally granted and there should be no restriction on the size of the tenements. According to the Steering Group out of 197 cases pending under this section, 182 are of holdings below 10,000 m^2 which means, as per the recommendations of the group, that only 15 cases will remain under the purview of the Act if the group's recommendations are accepted.

Under the heading "other exemptions" the HPSG made two recommendations—the first being that employers proposing

to build tenements for industrial employees were to be exempted
and secondly, that persons seeking change of land from industrial to residential use should be granted total exemption. This
meant that the large tracts of vacant land in the industrial zones
in Bombay (mostly owned by industrialists) can escape the Act,
while at the same time, no guarantee exists that houses for the
poor will be built on the exempted plots.

Though the aims and objectives of the Act were to make land
available to genuinely poor sections, it has failed in this regard.
Since the day the Act was promulgated, the prices of land and
flats have shot up 300 per cent. This has proved to be quite
detrimental to the E.W.S. most of whom live in slums.

If these slum dwellers pay to the property owners compensation at the rate of Rs. 10/- per m^2 on the land (as offered by the
Government under the Act), each family will have to pay no more
than Rs. 200/- (assuming that the occupants have only 15 m^2
as dwelling space to which has been added another 40 per cent as
the family's share of roads and open space). However, as a consequence of the Vacant Lands Act the slum dwellers have to pay
Rs. 22/- as a monthly fine/compensation/penalty (which used to
be recorded as rent before the Vacant Lands Act came into being
in 1975). Considering that the UL (C & R) Act came into force
in 1976 the slum dwellers have already paid more than six times
the amount they would have to pay in order to become owners
of the occupied land under the provisions of the Act.

An exclusive report under the above heading appeared in
"The Daily" on Thursday, March 1, 1982: "The Act is being
drastically modified according to highly informed sources. The
announcement to this effect by the Union Government is expected
in the near future".

It also stated that the notification would amount to the
scrapping of the Act: "The high power central committee formed
by the Union Government has finally decided that the government was not capable of either enforcing the Act or building
houses on the acquired land if at all acquired".

This "drastic modification" or "scrapping" of UL (C & R)
Act will bring the curtain down on the tragicomedy that was
being enacted under the pretence of framing and implementing
progressive legislation.

In February 1982, Shri Bishma Narain Singh, the then Union

Works and Housing Minister, said that the Act would be amended to "curb speculation in view of the emphasis being placed on the 20-point programme on measures to arrest unwarranted increases in urban land prices." He told the housing ministers from those states attending the conference "that the public sector has only a marginal though promotional role to play in providing urban housing".

Thus the UL (C & R) Act that was introduced to curb speculation in keeping with the "lofty" aims of the 20-point programme is today being withdrawn for precisely the same reason.

In August 1982 a bill to amend Section 21 of the Tamil Nadu UL (C & R) Act 1979, empowering the government to grant any exemption with retrospective effect was introduced in the Tamil Nadu Legislative Assembly by the Revenue Minister. Section 21 of the Act did not allow for exemption retrospectively. Hence the amendment.

Afterwards, the then Works and Housing Minister, Shri P.C. Sethi, told newsmen that the government intends to introduce changes in the Act that "would go a long way in encouraging private housing".

In Bombay, since September 1980, applications for clearance started piling up, after the then Chief Minister A. R. Antulay sent a letter to the competent authority not to process files relating to Section 22. Applications under Section 21 were any way never sent to the C.A. and piled up in Mantralaya.

In fact, a writ petition was proposed to be filed by four associations—the Practising Engineers and Architects and Town Planners Association, the Builders, Developers and Promoters Association, the Association of Building Industries of Maharashtra and the Property Owners Association, in the High Court against the State Government, for the delay in clearing applications under the UL (C & R) Act. Having too much to hide, however, it is not surprising that nothing came of this petition.

Perhaps it was not necessary. From August 1982 the Government once again started granting NOCs liberally. It was announced by the Government in the Legislative Assembly that exemptions were granted under Section 22 to Pure Drinks Limited, Worli, to the extent of 17,000 m^2 and the Tata Oil Mills to the extent of 50,000 m^2. The then Chief Minister Bhosale also gave the following information to the Legislative Assembly that

NOCs to four parties in respect of land in excess of 10,000 m^2 were granted to: The Bombay Soap Factory, the Hindustan Candle Manufacturing Company, Akbar Ali Porbandarwalla and Mundaner Salts, to expand business and construct buildings. Eight hundred acres in the non-development zones were also exempted.

About 18,292 applications in all are pending with the Government today, out of which 8,291 applications have been cleared.

The Government justifies the current reversal of the earlier Government policy of not granting NOCs by arguing that it will cause flat prices to fall. On the contrary increased building activity will cause rise in prices since increase in supply of houses does in no way affect demand. Flat prices are determined by many factors besides the simple supply/demand equation. Nor is it correct to see the rise in the prices of flats over the last few years as being caused by the holding up of NOCs. Other reasons, specifically the new social use of land by high profit enterprises is the main cause of rising prices. Flat prices will now rise even steeper after the NOC's are liberally granted.

Finally, even if prices of flats do fall, this can at the maximum only benefit the middle and upper income groups at the expense of the poor who were supposed to have been housed on the vacant, surplus and acquired land under the Act. To further justify the liberalisation by saying that only 60 per cent of the land will be handed over to the private builders and the rest will be handled by the Government, or that a land tax will be levied, or that the Government will insist on smaller houses, or that the liberalisation is being done to stimulate private investment in housing are simply lies. The UL (C & R) Act was enacted precisely because the private sector had no interest in building houses for the poor, precisely because a land tax was not viable, precisely because what was in short supply was land, not money.

IV

This is the picture that emerges out of the mock-fight between the owners of the large tracts of vacant land in the city and the State Government authorities over the control and regulation of such lands. We have gone into such details relating to the ceiling and regulation of vacant land in Bombay to emphasise the fact that in the absence of a political will the Government cannot solve the accommodation problem that the members of euphemistically called economically weaker section (EWS) in the city face. The first essential step towards a rational housing policy in a city like Bombay would be total governmental control, without any ambiguity, on the vacant land in the city. The nexus that exists between the rich in the city on the one side and the upper level governmental bureaucracy and the politicians on the other belies any such possibility.

In the next chapter we will review the slum relocation and improvement programmes in the city.

NOTES

1. For details see *Bombay Metropolitan Region Development Authority Report*, 1976 (Mimeographed).
2. See Draft Fifth Five-Year Plan, 1974, Vol. II.
3. See Colin Gonsalves, *Requiem For An Act* on UL (C & R) Act, 1976, Planning Action Research Team, Yusuf Meherally Centre, National House, 6, Tulloch Road, Bombay-400 039, Oct. 1982.
4. See Colin Gonsalves, *Bombay : A City Under Seige*, ISRE, Bombay, 1981, for an excellent critique of the Kerkar Committee Report.

CHAPTER FOUR

SLUM IMPROVEMENT AND RELOCATION PROGRAMME : AN ASSESSMENT

I

In chapter two we discussed briefly the State Government's policy of slum clearance and noticed that the programmes relating to slum clearance and relocation of the poor in 'good' or 'better' houses ended in a whimper due to certain reasons. As we observed, the magnitude of resources required to build such houses and the financial incapacity of slum dwellers in the city to buy them or even to pay their market rent were the principal reasons behind the failure of the entire programme.

Here we propose to examine in some detail the programmes relating to slum 'improvement' and 'relocation' adopted by the State Government as some kind of a complementary line to slum clearance. We also propose to look at the consequences of such measures undertaken by the Government on the slum dwellers involved.

II

Programmes relating to the relocation and improvement of slums in Bombay as we find them now came into being along with 'The Maharashtra Slum Areas (Improvement, Clearance and Redevelopment) Act passed by the State Legislature in 1971. This Act was framed in line with the existing 'National Slum Clearance and Improvement' Act of 1956. The rationale behind

44

the 1971 Act was to make a better provision for the improvement and clearance of the slum areas in the State and their redevelopment. The main provisions of the Act can be summarised as below :

As per the Act, any area in the State which is unfit for human habitation would be declared a slum area and works of improvement would be carried out by the owner of the building or of the land on direction from the Authority. If the owner fails to execute the works of improvement, the Authority itself may enter and execute the works of improvement. Moreover, in case the Authority is convinced that demolition of building is the best way to deal with the matter, it may direct the owner to do so, failing which the Authority itself may enter and demolish the building and sell the materials thereof to meet the expenses. No person shall erect any building in the demolished area except with the express permission in writing of the Authority. However, the Authority shall as far as practicable secure accommodation in advance for housing those who may be dishoused as a result of the demolition.

The Authority may redevelop the clearance area at its own cost in the public interest. For this, the adjoining area may be acquired if found necessary.

No suit, prosecution or other legal proceedings shall be initiated against the Authority or against any person acting under its authority for anything which is in good faith done or intended to be done under the Act or the rules made thereunder.

This Act, as one can see, empowers the Government to declare particular slum colonies as unfit for human habitation and as dangerous or injurious to public health. This certification has widely been used to demolish and remove slums whenever the land was required for some so-called 'public purposes'. The Act, not in words but in intent and action, has marked the hundreds of thousands of people living in appalling health and sanitary conditions as posing a threat to "the citizen". (As if in the eyes of the Government these workers in the city are not the 'citizens' of the country.)

The other objective of the Act was redevelopment which meant some basic amenities to those slums certified as not dangerous or injurious to public health and fit for human habitation. The basic amenities included :

1. Street light at the rate of one pole per 100 families.
2. One WC seat for 20-50 persons depending on the availability of space.
3. One water tap for 150 persons.
4. Approach links to houses, common pathways and streets to be laid by realigning huts.
5. Re-laying gutters and drains.

As the Municipal records and some studies including the present one reveal, only a small section of the slum population in the city was covered under this programme. Bulk of the slum population remained without any amenities as provided for in the Act. As per Municipal records we have the following figures to show the extent of the amenities provided to the slum dwellers.

Table : showing provision of basic amenties during the years 1972-73 & 1973-74 to the slums in Bombay

1.	Sanctioned and completed projects during the specified period	...	120
2.	Number of people benefited	...	3,29,867
3.	Rupees spent (in lakhs)	...	21,388
4.	Number of WCs	...	5,115
5.	Number of water taps	...	2,838
6.	Number of street lights	...	531
7.	Gutter in metres	...	98,159
8.	Roads in square metres	...	2,05,372

Another legislation was introduced in 1973 namely "The Maharashtra Slum Improvement Board Act". This Act led to the emergence of a body to implement improvement works only for hutment colonies on the State Government and Municipal lands and that too only for such hutment colonies which were not earmarked for eviction in the city development plan. To quote from the Maharashtra Slum Improvement Act—"...Existing slums are becoming a source of danger to health, safety and convenience of the slum dwellers and also to the surrounding areas and generally a source of nuisance to the public...(and) *until such time as these slums are improved and the people re-housed*, it is necessary to provide basic necessities such as water. sanitary arrangements and electricity to them".

A co-ordinating body for the slum improvement programmes in the State, namely the Slum Improvement Board was set up in February, 1974. This Board with a large number of functionaries at different levels was now the principal executive organ of the State Government for implementation of the programme (see the organisation chart constructed overleaf).

We summarise here some of the crucial provisions of this Act which have a large bearing on the existence of slum dwellers in the city.

The Board shall carry out the improvement works, works of maintenance and repair, collect service charges, and all other works subject to the control, direction and superin-tendence of the State Government.

It *may as far as practicable* offer the dishoused alternative *sites in any area* (emphasis ours). If any occupier fails to vacate and to shift to the alternative site offered to him within the specified period, the responsibility of the Board to provide him with an alternative site shall cease.

Moreover, the Board *may use such force as may be reasonably necessary for the purpose of getting the premises vacated*, if any occupier does not vacate the premises (em-phasis ours).

It should be noted that there was a subtle but significant shift on the accent from "alternative accommodation" (as per Maharashtra Slum Areas Act, 1971) to "alternative site" (as per Maharashtra Slum Improvement Board Act, 1973). The armed police could be used now to demolish the hutments and any atrocity committed by them was not to be questioned in courts. Anything done as per the Act was to be taken now as something done in 'good faith' and 'public interest'.

As the subsequent developments have shown, the relocation and improvement programme in the State in general and Bombay city in particular has so far essentially been a programme of

ORGANIZATIONAL CHART

(The various functionaries involved in the Management of the Slum Improvement programmes)

STATE GOVERNMENT

(Overall Control)

Cabinet Sub-Committee
(Decision on Removal & Resettlement)

Secretary Housing

Controller of Slums (Regulation & Control of Slums)

Maharashtra Slum Improvement Board (Execution of Slum Improvement Works)

CEO (Execution of Slum Improvement Works directly)

Municipal Corps/Councils (Maintenance of Slum Improvement Works & Executing Agencies of Board)

M.H.B. (Executing Agency)

Additional Collector (Encroachment) State Government Lands

Bombay Muni. Corp. Ward Officers

Maharashtra Housing Board (Slums on Housing Board lands)

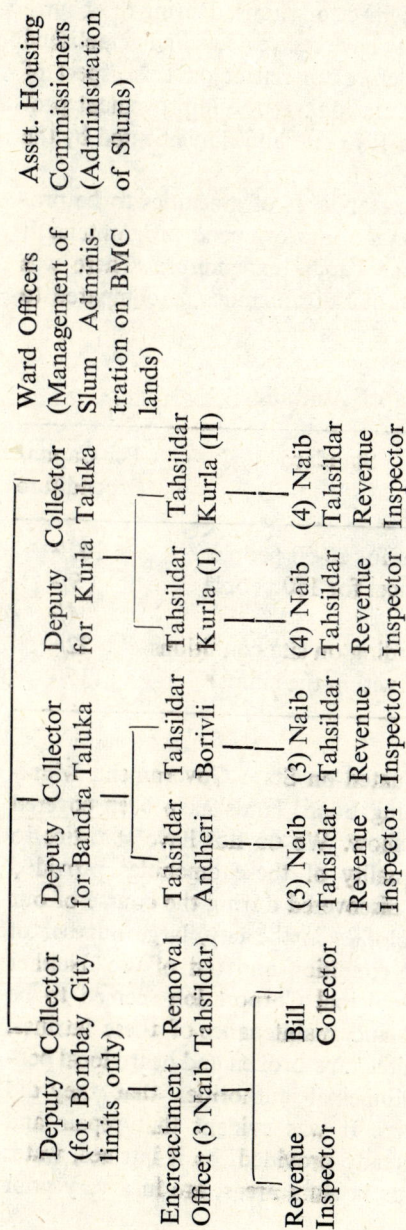

Asstt. Housing Commissioners (Administration of Slums)

Ward Officers (Management of Slum Administration on BMC lands)

Deputy Collector (for Bombay City limits only)

Deputy Collector for Bandra Taluka

Deputy Collector for Kurla Taluka

Encroachment Removal Officer (3 Naib Tahsildar)
- Revenue Inspector
- Bill Collector

Tahsildar Andheri — (3) Naib Tahsildar Revenue Inspector

Tahsildar Borivli — (3) Naib Tahsildar Revenue Inspector

Tahsildar Kurla (I) — (4) Naib Tahsildar Revenue Inspector

Tahsildar Kurla (II) — (4) Naib Tahsildar Revenue Inspector

thoughtless eviction and demolition of slums. During the course of last ten years slums in the city have been evicted and demolished on an unprecedented scale. Before we reflect on this aspect of urban development, let us have a look at the improvement programmes as formulated by the 1973 Act and implemented by the authorities.

The table below shows the standards of amenities to be provided to the slums taken under improvement programme. It also shows the estimated per capita expenditure. There was nothing new in 1973 Act in terms of amenities as compared to the provisions in 1971 Act.

Standards of Amenities

Sr. No.	Facility	Standard	Per Capita/ Expenditure
1.	Latrine	1 Seat for 20-50 people	100/-
2.	Water tap	1 Faucet for 150 people	9/-
3.	Street Light)		4/-
4.	Pathways)	depending on site conditions	22/-
5.	Drainage)	(only within the slums)	15/-

Majority of the slums situated on State Government, Municipal Corporation and Housing Board lands have been covered as the Government records show. We do not have statistics to show the extent and the quality of these amenities provided to the slum dwellers. As we discovered during the course of our visit to some of the slum colonies in the city, large number of latrines were in awfully bad condition and out of use. Neither the local people nor the Municipal Corporation seemed to be concerned about the repair and maintenance of these latrines. In several cases we found water taps broken and heard local people complaining against Municipal authorities that they did not care at all about repairs. It was evident that repair and maintenance of amenities already provided, be it latrines, water taps, drainage, or street lights in slum areas, are in a very poor state.

As pointed out above, the 1973 Act provides for improvement programme principally in the slums located on State Government, Municipal Corporation and Housing Board lands. Slums on private lands and in plots owned by governmental agencies like the Port Trust, Central Government and the Defence Services cannot be easily brought within the scope of "improvements". In case of private lands the procedure is a long winded one. After an area is declared as a slum under the SA (ICR) Act, 1971 the owners have a right to appeal to the Tribunal. If the area in question is deemed fit for improvement by the Tribunal, the matter is handed over to BHADB, which then proceeds with the execution of the improvement programmes. In the city so far around 542 out of 780 slum pockets on private lands have been declared as slums. Out of these 542 appeals for 272 pockets have been received. Of the remaining 270 pockets 141 have been administratively approved by BHADB. In terms of actual implementation of the improvement programme, as the records show, upto 1980 only 23 slum pockets had been able to obtain amenities like water, electricity and toilet facilities. Why such complicated procedures? Why so much of indecision and delay? It is not simply the red-tapism for which our bureaucracy is notorious. It should also be kept in mind that giving basic amenities amounts to an indirect recognition of 'illegal' occupants. The vested interests would, naturally, like to delay it as much as possible.

On Central Government land so far no improvement works have been undertaken as according to Central Government Properties Act of 1948, State laws do not apply to Central Government land and the various Central Government authorities have got other uses in mind for these lands and are not willing to improve existing slums. The Defence Services, for example, may need their lands for some specific use at any time, though in practice plots of many governmental agencies are lying unused for many decades.

Now let us have a look at the expenditure side of the slum improvement programme in the city. We present below the figures and the clarifications on the same as presented in the reports prepared by relevant authorities.

The Government has so far spent Rs. 171.5 million covering a population of about 1.50 million in Greater Bombay. The following table shows annual expenditure on environmental improvement and population covered.

Annual Expenditure on Slum Improvement

Year	Investment (Rs. in million)	Population covered (In lakhs)
1974-75	10.72	2.94
1975-76	45.30	5.85
1976-77	38.36	4.79
1977-78	33.17	2.95
1978-79	21.19	n.a.
1979-80	10.36	2.25

It may be seen from the above table that the investment has consistently gone down from 1975-76 onwards. Further, the implementing agencies are of the opinion that in the slum pockets where improvements are to be carried out immigration has been at higher rate as these slums have become more attractive.

Moreover, the implementing agencies face the difficulties in acquiring even a small piece of land for Acqua-Privy blocks, water taps etc., and the problems of shifting positions of those huts which come in the way of pathways etc.

The legislation provides for levy of compensation and service charges for provision of facilities varying according to the size of the hut. This is indicated in the following table :

Service Charges in Improved Slum

Sr. No.	Area of hutment (including open site encroachment)	Rates to be charged per hut per month
1.	Up to 14 sq. m. (approx. 150 sq. ft.)	Re. 1/- +adm/service charges of Rs. 10/-*
2.	Between 14 sq. m. & 23 sq. m. (approx. 250 sq. ft.)	Rs. 5/-+10 paise per sq. ft. over 14 sq. m.+10 service/ adm. charges i. e. Rs. 25/-

3.   Over 23 sq. m.   Rs. 5/- for first 14 sq. m.+25 paise over 14 sq.m.+Rs. 10/-*

---

*Out of Rs. 10/-, 9/- are Municipal charges for service provided and maintained by B.M.C. and Re. 1/- is to be retained by each land owning authority for adm. purposes.

The varying rates charged are to be collected and debited to the fund created for this purpose. B.M.C. has to maintain the facilities out of Rs. 9/- per hut that they recover. Apart from this, for huts with semi-permanent or permanent structures B.M.C. has the right to levy their usual Municipal taxes. The arrears in payment of these dues, however have been large, with the result that B.M.C. is not able to maintain the facilities in the slum pockets and they soon deteriorate beyond use. Further in case of private lands, collection of the compensation is an issue under discussion and hence facilities in hutments on private lands are not maintained at all.

In January 1982 the per capita expenditure on the amenities was revised and raised to Rs. 200/- from Rs. 150/-. The Municipal Corporation started collecting Rs. 20/- as service charges without considering whether all promised services were provided. Part of this amount goes towards the maintenance of the land etc. and part is reserved for expenses on eviction in future. Slum dwellers are supposed to pay for their own eviction.

Looking at the above problem of maintenance, especially in case of latrines, BHADB has come up with a new idea of distributing AP Blocks of small size at the norm of one latrine per 20 persons for a smaller cluster of huts hoping that with such arrangements the maintenance and use of AP blocks would improve.

The environmental improvement programme thus has not been able to fully succeed in its objectives due to various factors. The vast size of slum population poses operational and financial difficulties and whatever work is being done is not being maintained due to the problem of recovery of service charges. No monitoring and evaluation is done once the facilities are provided, and thus when population increases in an improved slum proportionate increase in facilities does not take place overburdening the existing services.

The problem of recovery is not simply due to low incomes of the people though this is a very important reason. It is also probably due to the psychological feeling of insecurity and of being the marginal population. In absence of security of tenure, the slum dwellers are reluctant to pay even for the utilities.

III

As pointed out earlier what has emerged as a fact more prominently out of the execution of the 1971 and 1973 Acts discussed above is demolition and eviction of slums in the city than their improvements. A review of the so-called relocation and redevelopment programmes based on the provisions of the abovementioned Acts would reveal it very clearly.

In principle the evicted slum dwellers under the Acts were to be located on new sites with some basic facilities provided there. The 'Site and Service' programme was devised to meet this need. According to this programme pitches with open drainages, street lights, main approach road, public toilets and watertaps were set up in the areas like Shivaji Nagar (Govandi) and Malvani (Malad). Hutment dwellers evicted from some densely populated pockets in the city were forced to go to these areas. Those who went were issued identity cards which said that they had no right to the land they occupied and that they 'may be' evicted whenever the place was required for some 'higher need' than their housing. They were provided with spacious 15' × 20' pitches, 4' × 15' lane between houses with the 'mori' (drain) in the centre of the lane. One main road 3.65 mts., i.e., about 12 ft. wide was built in every area to provide access for police vans, fire engines, sewage cleaning vans and ambulances etc.

These new sites as shown on paper appeared quite attractive. But the actual physical condition in which these sites existed was appalling. Some of the local newspapers carried the reports narrating the use of brutal force in demolishing and evicting slums one after another. Some of them also carried the reports on the actual physical conditions obtaining on the new sites (see some of these reports reproduced in a separate section below).

Only a tiny section of the evicted slum dwellers have so far gone to these sites. In fact locating sites has itself been a problem for the government and the Municipal authorities. In actual operation, thus, these slum dwellers have been left to themselves. Obviously they have not left the city. They are squatting again there itself or somewhere else in the city in a much wretched condition.

Taking advantage of these Acts (1971 and 1973) owners of the private lands on which slums were located started demolishing and evicting them on an unprecedented scale. This led to a number of protests organised by different political groups mainly in opposition on behalf of the affected slum dwellers. Private land owners were made the chief target. The Government of Maharashtra issued an Ordinance subsequently as a supplementary to the 1973 Act. The Ordinance stated that '..legal proceedings for evicting an occupier from any building or land in slum areas cannot be taken without the permission of the "competent" authority. On the face of it the Ordinance looked progressive and it was there to give protection to the slum dwellers from any arbitrary and summary eviction. But, in effect, obtaining the 'permission of the competent authority' did not pose much problem to the landlords. It was easier for them to obtain such permission and evict slum dwellers from their huts without having any liability in terms of providing the evicted slum dwellers with any alternative accommodation. Eviction had a legal sanction now.

The growing resistance of workers in the hutment colonies against eviction and lack of basic amenities called for another piece of legislation. During emergency, "The Maharashtra Vacant Lands (prohibition of unauthorised structures and summary eviction) Act 1975" was introduced. The purpose of the Act was to prohibit the unauthorised occupation of 'Vacant land' in the urban areas of the state and to provide for summary eviction of persons from such lands on the grounds, once again, that they were causing grave danger to public health, sanitation and disturbing the peaceful life of the inhabitants of the area concerned.

According to this Act, all such lands on which hutments and slum colonies have come up can be declared vacant and following such declaration those who occupy them will be treated as unauthorised occupiers. The Act gives arbitrary and summary powers of eviction to the government. The courts cannot be moved against these evictions and resisting eviction is a cognisable and unbailable offence. Private landlords are prohibited from evicting any slums from their land—State is there to do it for them. Even before the Act was finally passed, eviction of 70,000 people of Janata colony and their forcible removal to Cheeta Camp, a marshy low-lying area near Trombay had taken place with the help and intervention of armed police just before few days of onset of monsoon over the city (see the chapter on Janata Colony).

With the help of the very Vacant Lands Act, a total of 7,500 huts were demolished in different parts of the city just before the monsoon of 1979. These evicted hutment dwellers including residents from Cuffe Parade hutment area of Bombay were thrown to Malvani—a distance of about 45 kms away from the city in the western suburbs (see the section on Malvani slum dwellers). Soon after the monsoon of 1979, demolition of another 45,000 hutments was authorised, but fortunately the arrival of forthcoming Municipal and Assembly elections spared the dwellers of these hutments of the city. Soon after the elections eviction and demolition started. During the course of last three years thousands of slum huts and pavement dwellings have been demolished and the occupants driven away. The city newspapers have been carrying out the eviction and demolition reports from time to time. According to one such report published on July 24, 1983 in The Sunday Observer, between January 1 and April 30 that year alone as many as 11,853 unauthorised hutments were detected of which 9,851 were demolished without any provision for their alternative accommodation.

Large scale evictions do not mean that thousands of huts are demolished on a single day or two. Pockets are chosen and the demolition spread out over a period so as to avoid organized resistance. There were instances of burning of the hutment colonies which were authorised for demolition under this Act, e.g., Baiganwadi slums in Govandi area. It was an easy and quick way to demolish 4,000 huts in a record time.

The Municipal Corporation of Greater Bombay has constituted a permanent "demolition squad" in order to evict hutment colonies that come up in every Municipal ward—each manned by *Five* municipal senior staff members, *Two* sub-inspectors of Police, *Twenty-Five* police constables, *Twenty-Five* labourers and provided with *Two Lorries* to confiscate the slum dwellers belongings. The incurred expenditure towards this 'demolition squad' is estimated to be Rs. 10 lakhs per month or Rs. 1.20 crores a year. The Municipal Corporation laments the lack of funds for providing basic amenities like drinking water, sanitation to the slum dwellers but is prepared to spend this large amount to destroy thousands of hutments every year. Demolition expenses of every hutment is fixed at the rate of Rs. 60/- as per the provisions of the Act and is collected from the evicted families.

The Government of Maharashtra has followed the same procedure to demolish all so-called 'unauthorised' structures (basically workers' colonies and slum areas) by formulating a 'demolition cell' under the direct supervision of a senior government officer, of the level of Dy. Controller of Slums with assistance of Police force, SRP and labourers working for municipal corporation, to pull down the 'unauthorised structures' on the 'Vacant Lands'.

Some landlords in the city subsequently challenged the validity of the Maharashtra Vacant Lands Act in court. They questioned the Government's right to collect rent from their private property and declare private land as vacant land. The Bombay High Court passed a verdict in favour of landlords, in February 1980 and held that the Act was unconstitutional and confiscatory in nature. Since the elections were approaching, different political groups rallied round the hutment dwellers to protest against the judgment.

This enabled the Government to start propaganda that it would 'protect' the slum dwellers from landlords and to issue an ordinance reinstating the main provisions of the Maharashtra Vacant Lands Act, restoring to the Government the power to carry out summary evictions. The Ordinance was issued by the Government on March 6, 1980. It is significant to note that within less than two weeks of this measure supposedly intended to protect slum dwellers, the Bombay Municipal Corporation carried out a massive demolition operation, as mentioned earlier, ruthlessly burning down the huts. Private land owners have again challenged the ordinance before the court. Thus the tussle between two sets of landlords—the Government and private property owners—continues with tens of lakhs of people living in Bombay's slums as pawns in the game.

In the year 1977, the Bombay Housing Board of 1948, the Bombay Building Repairs and Reconstruction Board (BHB, BBRRB) 1969 and The Maharashtra Slum Improvement Board of 1973 were dissolved. A new body came into existence with the introduction of the Maharashtra Housing and Area Development Act 1977. As a result, the new body, Maharashtra Housing and Area Development Authority with its planned efforts and centralised control, through its four regional Boards at Bombay, Pune, Nagpur and Aurangabad is charged with the responsibility of the implementation of the schemes of the Government to tackle the crisis on the housing front.

Under the British, the Bombay Government restricted its planning to rigid zoning regulations and effective segregation of the rich and the poor (the Backbay reclamation earmarked for the former, and the 'native quarters' for the latter). The same emphasis on rigid zoning continues to be there, though in a new form, in the development plans.

These rules (plans) have not been framed on the basis of any clear set of actual requirements for the efficient management of the city's economy or the actual requirements of Bombay's population. Improbable standards are set for amenities and since these cannot be met, it obviates the need for providing any amenities at all. For instance, the zoning laws stipulate a minimum plot size of 330 sq. metres, far larger than any house the poor can afford. Fifteen per cent of the plot must be open. The maximum permissible density is of 100 plots per net acre. Building plans must be designed by architects, and must be implemented by the contractors. All these regulations can only permit flats and bungalows which the poor—and an increasing proportion of the middle classes—cannot afford.

One can see the Government's refusal to recognise the rights of the poor in a number of its actions relating to the relocation and improvement programmes. So far the slum upgradation programmes have given no right to shelter: the Slum Areas Act, the Vacant Lands Act and the MHADA offer no security of tenure whatsoever. Nor do the slum census identity cards:—
"This document does not confer any right on the occupant in

the property he has occupied", states each card. The Bombay
Municipal Corporation even prevents people from improving
their accommodation; it provides permission for repairs only
subject to the condition that "the temporary nature of the hutment shall be retained."

IV

The arbitrary and irrational manner in which the governmental
and municipal authorities have been going on with their programme of physically removing nearly half the city's population
from the pavements and slum colonies all over the city has arou-
sed the conscience of certain civil and democratic rights organisations in the city. For over a year now, a protracted legal battle
has been going on in the Supreme Court between the advocates
of such organisations and the Government of Maharashtra, the
Bombay Municipal Corporation and the Commissioner of Police,
Bombay, over the issue of demolition and eviction of pavement
and slum colonies. The petitioners on behalf of pavement dwellers have moved the country's highest court to save the city's
such poor who can afford shelter only on pavements and whose
physical survival is at stake in face of demolition and eviction.
The arguments advanced are that since the State Government
and the Municipal Council have disclaimed any responsibility
towards the consequences of eviction, failed to provide affordable
shelter, not acquired surplus urban land to release it to pavement
dwellers, and have failed to curb speculation in urban land and
housing, its action of eviction and demolition is highly unrea-
sonable depriving the poor of their right to life.

In their arguments the petitioners have pointed out that the
State which has a monopoly over land has failed to provide land
or housing to slum and pavement dwellers. This violates the
fundamental right of a citizen to have shelter. They have further
pointed out that the city has such vacant land where the poor
can be housed, and that the Government's plea of lack of financial resources is untenable. Reviewing the urban land and housing situation in the city and making it explicit that there is no
provision of affordable land or shelter for low-income groups,
the petitioners have pleaded with the Court to direct the State
Government to either provide shelter or make land available to

pavement and slum dwellers. They have also submitted that
such land must be close to the place of work and its rent must be
affordable. Further, they have pleaded for a mandatory order
and injunction from the Court preventing the Government and
the Municipality from evicting pavement dwellers and demolishing their huts.

Though the petitioners' accent is on pavement dwellers, the
whole dispute concerns the lives of the slum dwellers in the city.
Its ramifications have far-reaching consequences. As the petitioners' submission points out, the desire of the government to
demolish all hutments on pavements and slum colonies will result
in rendering over fifty per cent of the city's population homeless. In their arguments they have held that there has been a
total mismanagement of urban land causing the present chaotic
situation in the city.

The Supreme Court has so far been receptive to the petitioners'
arguments and quite severe and critical of the actions of the State
Government in Maharashtra. It has issued interim orders to
stop such arbitrary demolition and eviction.

The Supreme Court's orders seem to have alerted the governmental and civic authorities. The Government has just released
a draft development plan which is under attack by even those
who have supported the Government's policies against slum and
pavement dwellers. It is a fragmented draft plan covering only
the island city. The Government has also passed a new ordinance
amending the Maharashtra Regional Town Planning Act, 1966
to 'arm' itself 'sufficiently' to deal with 'unauthorised development'. The ordinance makes squatting and encroachment a
cognizable offence and states that arrests can be made without
a warrant. As one perceptive writer has put it, this ordinance
is an 'Unlawful Law'.[1]

NOTES

1. For an analysis of this ordinance see Kannam Srinivasan,
   'An Unlawful Law', Economic and Political Weekly Vol.
   XVIII, No. 6, June 25, 1983.

CHAPTER FIVE

FIELD-STUDY

(A) THE FOUR SLUMS

As mentioned in the Introduction, this social enquiry incorporates a field study of some selected slums in the city. In fact the whole project began with the sole idea of intensive field work in selected slums of the metropolis to find out the quality of life in relocated and improved slums. Later on, after the field work was over, it was realised that mere statistical presentation on the social origins of the slum dwellers, their health and living conditions, their experience with actions of eviction etc. will not guide us far in terms of an understanding of the whole process of 'relocation and improvement of slums' in the city. Decisions and actions relating to eviction, relocation and improvement of particular human settlements in a city are inextricably linked with the resources available and the way these resources are allocated. Decisions regarding allocation of resources, in turn, depend upon the phenomenon of power—economic and political power. In whose hands this power lies and how they exercise and use it are the questions which need answer for a fuller understanding of the problems relating to relocation and improvement of slums in a city.

We, therefore, decided to discuss the situation relating to the growth of slums in the city, planning process and the slum problem, the housing situation in the city, availability or non-availability of the vacant land for rehabilitating the poor in the city, and the operation of the different programmes of relocation, improvement etc. of the slums in the city along with the field study undertaken. We think that the abovementioned

61

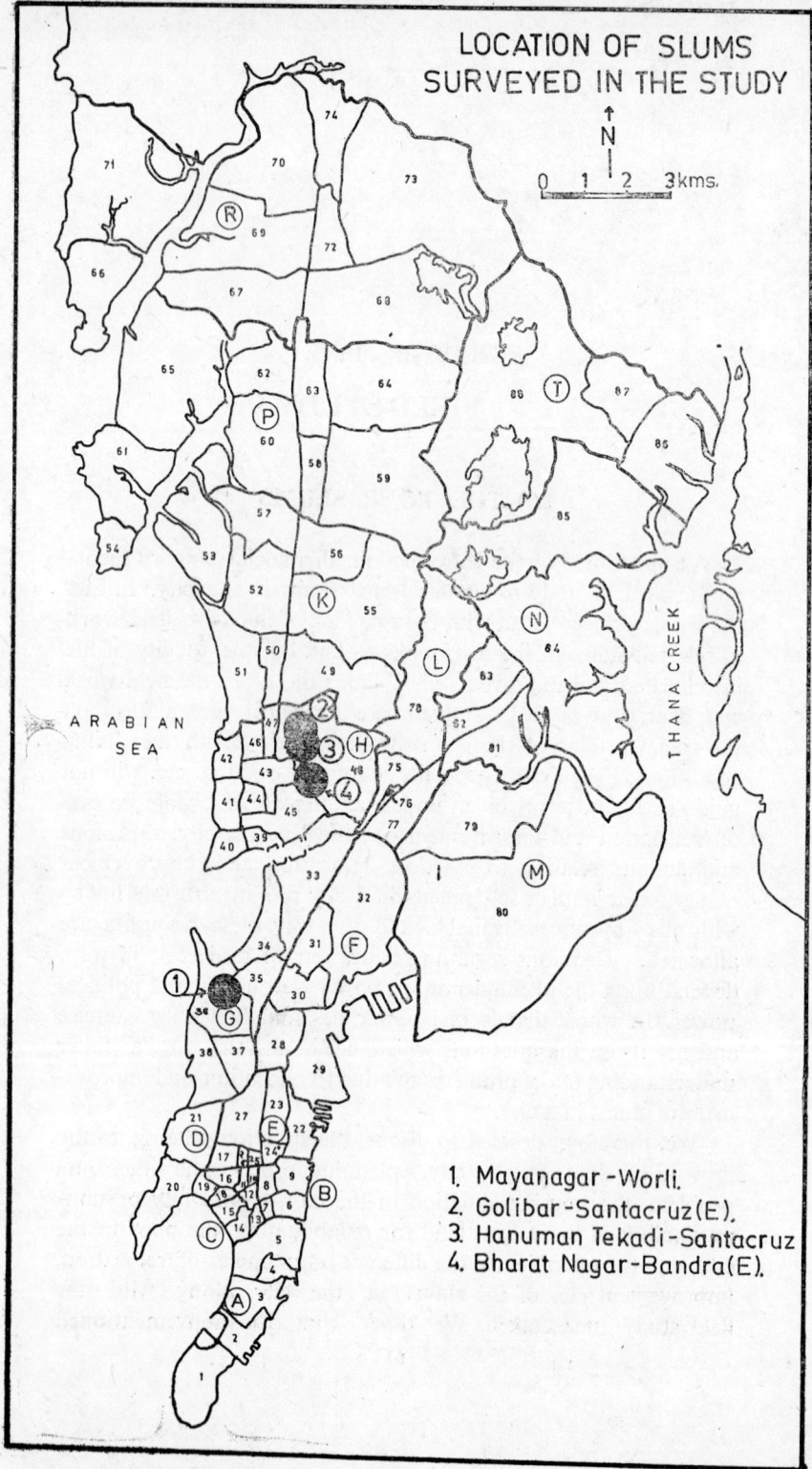

LOCATION OF SLUMS
SURVEYED IN THE STUDY

↑
N

0 1 2 3kms.

ARABIAN SEA

THANA CREEK

1. Mayanagar-Worli.
2. Golibar-Santacruz(E).
3. Hanuman Tekadi-Santacruz
4. Bharat Nagar-Bandra(E).

issues are vitally interlinked with the phenomenon of economic and political power and this manifests clearly when the question of housing the poor in the city arises.

The preceding four chapters deal with such issues keeping in view the process of administrative decision-making in the city. What follows here is basically a statistical narration of the data obtained through a field work done in four slums of Bombay in 1978.

I

The four slums selected for our field study were Bharat Nagar, Hanuman Tekdi, Golibar and Maya Nagar. We wanted to have in our sample 'relocated' and 'improved' slums. Our selection of these four slums can only be called arbitrary. Slums abound in the city of Bombay. There are hundreds of such hut-ment colonies and we did not have enough facilities to work out a proper and useful classification of these pockets located at distant places in the city proper and Greater Bombay. So we put our convenience in reaching and working in a slum as the major criterion of selection. These slums, we found, met our twin criteria of physical convenience and the types. And, there-fore, we decided to conduct the study in the above noted slums. We have already mentioned in the introduction about the method of sampling etc. We have also mentioned that there is separate study of slum women included in this report. Why and how did we conduct this inquiry is explained in the introduction. This study of slum women will follow the main study.

II

BHARAT NAGAR

Bharat Nagar, a relocated slum, stretches over the land in Kurla Bandra complex not very far from the Bombay University campus at Kalina, accommodating an estimated population of about 15,000 (fifteen thousand) people as of 1977-78. It is a sprawling and growing slum as one can see it visiting at inter-vals. Originally, the residents, part of them, lived at Kherwadi in Bandra, not very far from the present location. Nearly eight years ago Kherwadi was demolished and the people evicted were given shelter at the place named as Bharat Nagar.

According to the information given by a local resident, in early 1950s there were nearly sixty to seventy huts in Kherwadi, all belonging to the Harijans. B.G. Kher who was then the Chief Minister of Bombay claimed to have worked among these Harijans, and on his request Pandit Jawaharlal Nehru visited the area. After his visit the place was named after Mr. Kher as Kherwadi. Kherwadi, as stated above, was evicted some years ago and the people were given option to settle at the new place called Bharat Nagar.

Bharat Nagar is a much different place now as compared to Kherwadi of early fifties. It does not inhabit only Harijans. There are Muslims who dominate the area equally, if not more. Besides Harijans and Muslims there are several other castes present in the area. Majority of the Harijans are employed as sweepers and scavengers in the Municipal Corporation, the railways and the housing societies etc. The Muslims work in the slaughter house at Deonar, have their petty trades and are engaged in various kinds of services. Others earn their living through employment in industries mostly as unskilled labour and also by working for jobs in the informal sector.

Bharat Nagar has a very 'bad' image among the people living in its neighbourhood. 'It is a place of smuggling, gambling, illegal liquor trade, prostitution and crime'; 'A large scale illegal liquor trade takes place in the open pitches behind the Bombay University campus'; 'Matka dens are common in the slum'; 'Pimps throng the area during the day and night, and quite often, young ladies and girls are taken to the city to please the oil-rich Arabs on tour of the city'. These are some of the most common remarks passed on Bharat Nagar by the people residing outside the colony. Our investigators were forewarned by some of them whom they happened to meet during the course of the field work, to be cautious while moving in the area. Experience of our investigators (two of them were girls), however, was much different. They never felt any danger and were able to communicate with the residents without any difficulty once they were introduced to them by a local leader. About anti-social, illegal and criminal activities in the area, their observation was, however, not of a negative kind. Some residents of the area told them on their own that there were some individuals and also families in the colony which earned a 'bad' name for their community through their involvement in 'wrongful' activities. We did not attempt to measure the extent of unlawful activities in the area as this was not on the agenda of our research.

HANUMAN TEKDI

Hanuman Tekdi is a part of a huge slum called Golibar lying on the eastern side of the railway track between Khar and Santacruz stations. The Western Express Highway forms its eastern boundary. Golibar can be broadly divided into three spatial groupings: Golibar Society area, Hanuman Tekdi and a third area identified by the local population as the 'Bhaiya' Nagar or 'Bhaiya' area. We did the survey work in the entire Golibar society area. These slum pockets are claimed as areas where some improvement works have been done. We will first describe briefly the distinctive features of Hanuman Tekdi and then of Golibar Society.

Hanuman Tekdi derives its name from a small Hanuman temple in the area and is situated on the land belonging to the Defence Services. Originally occupied by a few ex-Servicemen, it did not take much time for it to grow into a large slum.

Hanuman Tekdi is dominated by neo-Buddhists who live in the southern part of the slum and prefer to call it Buddha Nagar. There is a Buddha temple in it with the figure of the Buddha and a large photograph of Dr. Babasaheb Ambedkar.

Besides neo-Buddhists there are Marathas, Kunbis, Kamatis, Muslims, Christians, Wadaris and Hindi-speaking people called Bhaiyas. The area is clearly dominated by the Marathi-speaking people.

Interesting thing about the area is the formation of clusters based on religion and caste. For instance, the Kamatis, Wadaris and Muslims have attempted to create neighbourhoods of their own.

Occupational structure of the area is highly heterogeneous. Work in industries at semi-skilled and unskilled levels seems to be the major type of employment for the people living in this area. There are varieties of jobs, ranging from driving a taxi or a private car to working as vendors, peons, watchmen, doing petty business etc., that the people of the area are engaged in to earn their living. It was noticed during the field work that quite a number of young men, approximately within the age group of 20 to 25 living in the area did not have any jobs. We did not measure the extent of unemployment either in Hanuman Tekdi or in other parts of Golibar, but it was evident that unemployment was a common phenomenon in the entire area.

GOLIBAR

'Golibar' means firing of bullet. This area was once a military firing range and, therefore, when it was transformed into a living place it was very conveniently called Golibar. Some years ago (the year is not known to us but not in a very distant past) it ceased to be used by the Military. Soon it was encroached upon by the homeless people in the city and it grew into a slum. Between 1949 and 1951 the State Government authorities declared the huts as illegal construction and issued orders to forfeit them. Later the authorities agreed to allow the people to live there provided they formed themselves into a co-operative housing society and sent proposals for grant of land in a prescribed manner within a stipulated period. Later on, as the Record of Rights at the Bombay Suburban Development Collector's office says, the authorities passed on the land to the Maharashtra Housing Board. This was done, as per the Record of Rights, because the Golibar Housing Society failed to make an application for grant of land in the prescribed manner within the period allowed. The Golibar Housing Society moved the High Court challenging the above decision of the authorities.

Golibar today is not the Golibar of early sixties. It has grown into a very large slum inhabiting Hindus, Muslims, Christians and neo-Buddhists speaking different languages and dialects and hailing originally from different parts of the country. As stated above it includes Hanuman Tekdi and Bhaiya Nagar. Our survey covered selected households in the Golibar Society and Bhaiya Nagar both.

Golibar Society area is an admixture of brick-built structures and shacks of the most fragile type. The former belong to the members of the Society and the latter to those who entered there as squatters.

The sector inhabited mainly by the Hindi-speaking people called as *Bhaiyas* by the outsiders, comprises mostly of the hutment-type structures. This sector has also people of other communities like *Kamatis*, Muslims, Christians and Maharashtrians. All these communities have separate aggregations generally identified as colonies. For example, the area occupied by the Maharashtrians is called by 'outsiders' as the Maratha colony who migrated here from another slum in the city.*

MAYA NAGAR

This was the fourth and the last slum covered in our survey. This was also the smallest slum as compared to the other three slums described above.

It is a compact slum lying near the Worli sea-face accommodating nearly three hundred hutments. This slum came into existence in the year 1960 as an effort to rehabilitate famine-striken people from Sangamner in Ahmednagar district of the State.

Majority of the residents in this slum are neo-Buddhists engaged in the conservancy services of the Municipal Corporation as sweepers and scavangers. Nearly all of them belong to the downtrodden section of the society and there is hardly any representation here of upper caste families. There is, thus, almost zero diversity in terms of caste, creed and language.

As stated above majority of the woking hands in the slum are employed as sweepers and scavangers. Some are engaged in textile mills mostly as unskilled workers. There are number of boys who work in small hotels and canteens as cleaners and waiters.

Compared to the average hutment in other slums in our sample, Maya Nagar dwellings have, by and large, better structure. The material used for construction appears to be of a better variety. This is supposed to be a slum where some improvement measures have been taken. Some huts have been re-built with better quality materials. Drains have been dug for unwanted water to be drained away. Water Scarcity in this slum is not that acute as it is in the other three slums described above.

*A detailed account of the entire Golibar is available in a book entitled "A Profile of an Indian Slum" by A.R. Desai and S.D. Pillai, University of Bombay publication (1972),

(Hanuman Tekdi being in the worst condition).

The slum is, however, not without problems. In the course of our field survey we discovered that residents of the area live under a threat of insecurity. Several slum women told our lady investigator that there was lot of sex crime in the area and that their movement after sunset was very unsafe. They reported about three rape cases in the area. As they stated there were some 'bad characters' living inside who helped outside 'goondas' to commit this type of crime.

We also came to know that as these dwellings are of a better quality they fetch a high price offered by people from 'outside'. As they reported, quite a number of better-built huts were traded for money in favour of certain 'landlords' and subsequently rented out to people from outside.

Recently a fairly strong group of Dalit movement activists has emerged in the area and it appeared the members of this group were determined to check the criminal activities in the locality.

III

What follows below is an aggregated profile of the four hundred households surveyed in the four slums described above.* Distribution of the sample was as below :

Bharat Nagar	:	140	Households
Golibar Colony	:	80	,,
Hanuman Tekdi	:	118	,,
Maya Nagar	:	62	,,
Total		400	

In fact in all nearly five hundred households were covered. But as answers were incomplete in several schedules and we doubted the work of the two investigators who came to us almost towards the end of the field work, we decided to take for tabulation only those interview schedules which were fully completed and checked. The total of such schedules came to four hundred and ten. Our

*All the tables presenting the data are put in Appendix. These tables show the data slnm-wise.

final decision was to tabulate the answers from four hundred.

*   *   *   *   *

MIGRATION PATTERN

What were the reasons that led to our respondents' migration to Bombay ? Nearly 61 per cent came here seeking employment. They did not have any means of livelihood in their native place. This is a well-known fact. To a very large extent urban poverty is a spill-over of rural poverty. Nearly 15 per cent said that they had some property at home but they were 'surplus member' there and therefore, migrated here in search of better prospects. For nearly 12 per cent Bombay was their 'home'. They were born here. For nearly 3 per cent the work of an agricultural labour was 'highly oppressive' and that is why they left their place. Nearly 6 per cent left their native place to escape 'debt' and 'bondage'. For almost each of them it was a 'family' debt and bondage which 'did not seem to come to an end'. They feared that they and their children 'will ever be in debt and bondage'. They, therefore, 'ran away' from their native place. For four persons in the total sample, social life at native place was 'oppressive' and that led to their movement out from there. One person holding a job said that he was transferred to Bombay and as he could not rent a place anywhere else, he came to stay in Hanuman Tekdi.

Which are the states they have migrated from ? Nearly 38 per cent of the total respondents were from the different parts of Maharashtra. Nearly 23 per cent came from Uttar Pradesh, 16 per cent from the Punjab and about 8 per cent from Andhra Pradesh. 4 per cent migrated from Gujarat and 3 per cent from Tamil Nadu. Little less than 3 per cent belonged to Karnataka by birth. Six persons said they were from Delhi. Four each from Madhya Pradesh and Goa and three from Bihar figured in our sample. There were two each from Kerala and Nepal and one each from West Bengal and Orissa. It was some kind of a surprise to find one family migrating from Pakistan and now living in Golibar.

It is really interesting to find that these slums have people from as many as fourteen states in the country and also from neighbouring States like Nepal and Pakistan. They are a micro-cosm of the unity called India.

What has been the period of their stay in various places ? Mobility, forced physical mobility, seems to be a very important element in the migration pattern in case of slum dwellers. Not only that they move out from their native place to settle down finally at some place in a city/town, they are generally compelled to move from one place to the other in a city/town and most of the time, as our data indicate, such compulsion arises out of eviction and demolition of their living place.

Of 379 persons who responded to the question mentioned above (21 persons did not respond) as many as 234 persons left their native place before they were 20 years of age. The break-down of this figure is as below :

> Fourteen persons were very young (1-5 years) when they left their native place (presumably with their parents); 26 persons were between 6 and 10 years of age at the time of migration from the native place; 71 were between 11 and 15 at the time of their first move-out, and 123 of them were between 16 and 20 at the time of their migration from the place of their birth. ·

Thirty-five of the respondents said that they left their place of birth when they were above 30 years of age. 73 persons were between 21 and 25 and 37 were between 26 and 30 years at the time of migration.

According to these figures the first migration takes place at a relatively younger age (196 persons in the sample between 16 and 25 years of age) which is quite understandable. This is the age (period) when search for employment and livelihood becomes most urgent and when a person is ready and also capable to take risks involved in distant migration. We do not mean to suggest that people above this age group cannot and do not take the risk of migration. In fact, compelled by adverse circumstances, they do migrate. But relatively speaking risk-taking capacity declines as the age advances.

As our data show, of 353 respondents (the remaining 26 out of 379 who responded to the first item on the question did not respond to the other items on the question) 262 settled with exactly one move from their place of birth, 54 had to have 2 moves, 18 moved thrice, 14 moved four times, and 5 persons moved exactly five times. Let us take the case of those who had just one move, i.e., those who moved directly from their native place to the present slum where they stay. Out of 262 such cases, 104 came in search of job (40%), 77 (nearly 30%) came here because of demolition at native place (another slum?).

What is the duration of their stay in Bombay? As many as 71 per cent of the total sample claimed that they were living in their respective slums for more than ten years. Nearly 14 per cent of them stated that they were in Bombay since their birth. Little over 10 per cent said that they were living in their slums for five to ten years and over 3 per cent said that they have been there for three to five years. Of the remaining 7 respondents 2 were there for one to three years and 5 for one year. (See the table in Appendix for slum-wise break-down of these figures. Bharat Nagar figures may be read with caution as this is a recently relocated slum. Perhaps they meant that they were in Kherwadi slum for all these years, the slum from where they were moved to Bharat Nagar).

What were the reasons for moving from place to place? Answers given to this question throw some light on the physical mobility pattern prevalent among the slum dwellers in this city which may also be the case elsewhere. As the data show (see the table in Appendix for details) inter-slum mobility tends to continue even after four moves though in a declining order. Whereas the first 'move-out' is generally caused by unemployment (in search of work from one slum to the other—nearly 30 per cent), demolition of hutments is the other important cause (22%) for the same. In our sample 77 persons (22%) were displaced once, 15 persons (22%) were displaced once, 15 persons twice, 4 persons thrice, 6 persons four times and 2 five times.

Keeping in view the very high incidence of eviction and demolition of slum colonies in the city, we feel our data do not picture very correctly the reality in this regard. The reason perhaps lies in the type of slums we undertook for our study. These slums would come in the category of 'safe' slums, if we can use the term 'safe' here. They are safe in the sense that two of them (Golibar colony and Hanuman Tekdi) are fairly long-settled slums having

acquired a relatively 'secure' status. They are fairly well established and politically protected slums. The ruling party, as of
the day, is quite active here. It will be very difficult for governmental authorities to uproot them. The other two slums (Bharat
Nagar and Maya Nagar) have also acquired more or less the
same status though for different reasons. Bharat Nagar inhabits
mostly the Harijans (sweepers and scavengers) and the Muslims,
two politically vulnerable minority communities. Maya Nagar
has mostly neo-Buddhists living there. One is a relocated slum
and the other a re-settled colony.

As our respondents are from these slums living there for a
considerable period of time, our data do not show much incidence of dislocation of the residents there causing flight from one
slum to the other which large number of other slums in the city
would show.

The figures obtained here show that nearly 17 per cent of
the respondents moved (majority of them only once) for business. As narrated in the beginning, quite a number of slum
dwellers in the city are self-employed. They are engaged in what
is identified as unorganised sectors, running small shops, providing different kinds of services and selling things as hawkers
in these areas.

Are they willing to go back to their native place? We asked
our respondents some questions to assess the possibility of *return-
migration* in their case. 363 out of the total number responded
to our questions showing their willingness/unwillingness to go
back to their native place (or the place of their ancestors in case
of those born here but responding to the questions). It is interesting to observe that little over 48 per cent of those who responded showed their willingness to go back to their native place.
41 persons of the 'willing' 175 were ready to move immediately
provided there was a sure prospect of employment there in the
form of either a 'permanent' job or 'some business'. Others
'desired' to go back to their native place for different reasons
like 'climatic and living conditions are better at native place'
(72), 'family is settled there' (28), 'have land and house (home)
there' (14), 'cost of living is much less in native place' (13), 'there
is always a threat of eviction and demolition in Bombay' (5),
and 'physical sickness and ill health in Bombay' (2).

For the remaining 52 per cent (of those who responded)

return-migration was not possible. Reasons being many: 'family is settled here in Bombay' (73), 'there are no employment prospects at native place (13), 'there are number of such prospects here in Bombay' (40), 'financial problems' (8), and 'accommodation problem' (8). Some were afraid of 'religious' (29) and 'political' (17) persecutions at native place. For them Bombay appeared to be a safe place to live.

SOCIAL AND DEMOGRAPHIC CHARACTERISTICS

Caste : The distribution of caste among 305 households, including 14 neo-Buddhists and 4 (four) tribal households, in our sample can be explained as follows :

Nearly 43.5 per cent of these households belonged to the members of the Scheduled Caste, little over 33 per cent to the category of 'others' (castes), nearly 18 per cent to the 'other backward communities' and 4 per cent to the members of the scheduled tribe.

The category 'others' (castes) in the sample remains unspecified. Which particular castes these households belonged to? As the main purpose of the study was to know the nature and consequences of eviction, relocation, improvement etc. of the slums in the city, not much attention was paid to the question/ questions pertaining to the caste, religion, family etc., of the respondents. Now we realise that some detailed information on such variables would have thrown additional light on the social composition of the slums surveyed. This would have helped us understand better the human situation in such areas. For example, it would be quite interesting to know whether upper caste (particularly Brahmin) families live in slums? If yes, what is the percentage of such families and how does it compare with lower caste/scheduled caste families' percentage. Do upper caste families (if they are there) live in very close proximity with lower caste families—in huts one upon other—in an urban environment? One can raise a host of such other questions.

We have included 14 households of neo-Buddhists in the category of scheduled caste. Existentially vast bulk of the neo-Buddhists in Maharashtra belong to this category.

There may not be any theoretical justification for including the members of the scheduled tribe in any caste-category, but existentially again, so far as these urban slums are concerned, there does not appear much difference, in cultural terms particularly, between them and the members of the lower castes sharing a slum life together.

Religion : Our sample of 400 households had a very large percentage of Hindus (approximately 72.5%). Muslims formed nearly 20 per cent, Christians nearly 4 per cent and neo-Buddhists nearly 3.5 per cent. There was a lone Sikh family in the sample.

It should be pointed out that Hindus dominate as a religious category only in three slums, namely Golibar colony, Hanuman Tekdi and Maya Nagar. Taken as a whole Bharat Nagar is dominated by Muslims. Predominance of Hindus as shown in our study is because of the aggregated percentage of the total sample. In the table on the distribution of families by religion (see Appendix) we have a slum-wise distribution of the sample. Our sample from Bharat Nagar was not representative so far as religious composition of this particular slum is concerned. Major concern here was to have the sample from those evicted from Kherwadi and relocated here.

Mother Tongue : There are at least twelve languages spoken in these slums. Hindi (41%) and Marathi/Konkani (32.5%) being the languages of nearly 74 per cent of the total households in the sample. The other nine languages spoken in these areas are Urdu, rather Hindustani (nearly 11%), Telugu (6.5%), Gujarati (3.5%), Kannada (2.5%), Malayalam (1.5%), Tamil (2 households), Nepali (2 households), Bengali (1 household) and Oriya (1 household).

FAMILY SIZE, AGE, SEX AND MARITAL STATUS

The average family size estimated was 4.42, slightly higher than the census figure, 4.38. The children's population (below the age of 16 years) constituted 40 per cent of the total. The population was male dominant with 843 females per 1000 males. 48 per cent of the total population came under the married category including two married children below the age of 16 years. Adults (16 years and above) formed 60 pent of the total population.

The most dominant age group was 1-10 years forming 28

per cent of the population. The age group (16-25 years) constituted 21 per cent, and of this 50 per cent were males.

The male/female ratio was 55 : 45 (approximately).

The survey brought out another fact, that subletting one
room to guests, usually natives, is quite common in slums. In
one case as many as nine guests were found living with the 'regular' dwellers. The 'resource person' who introduced the dweller
to the slum environment was found to be his relative. As observed by other studies, kinship, caste and religion are favourable
factors for migration. Same is the case here. The newcomers
from rural areas get acclimatized to the slum situation with
the help of their resource persons and fellow migrants.

OCCUPATIONAL STRUCTURE

Parental Occupation : An enquiry into the nature of parental
occupation of the respondents revealed that they came from families following different kinds of occupation: agriculture (42.5%),
manual labour (18%), trade and commerce (9%), manufacturing
(6%), service in industry (5.5%), personal services (4.5%),
landless labourer (4%), construction worker and domestic
servant (2% each), services in transport agency in case of three
respondents and in the department of water supply, electricity
etc., in the case of two. Twenty-two respondents did not specify
properly whether they were employed. Our guess is that they
were unemployed at the time of interview.

Respondent's Occupation, Sex and Income : Data obtained
on the nature of occupation (see Appendix) followed by our
respondents reveal that the slum dwellers whom the administrators and the members of the upper and the middle classes, in
general, living in the city consider as faceless members of a category of people, are in reality the workers whose services are
vitally essential for the existence of the city. In our enquiry we
found that these individuals were engaged in as many as thirty-
three types of jobs. We enumerate them below :

Sr. No.	Working as:	Male	Female	Total*
1.	Manual Labourer	90	6	96
2.	Peon, Watchman	32	nil	32
3.	Domestic Servant	2	21	23
4.	Clerk	24	nil	24
5.	Teacher	2	1	3
6.	Officer (not specified) ;	1	nil	1
7.	Bus Conductor	2	nil	2
8.	Postman	1	nil	1
9.	Inspector (Pharmaceutical)	1	nil	1
10.	Sweeper	53	15	68
11.	Social Worker (self-styled)	1	nil	1
12.	Washerman (Dhobi)	1	nil	1
13.	Salesman	2	nil	2
14.	Contractor (petty contract jobs like minor repairs etc.)	4	nil	4
15.	Black marketeer (perhaps selling illicit liquor)	1	nil	1
16.	Self-employed (petty shop-keeper, vendor, hawker, etc.)	50	3	53
17.	Textile Worker (unskilled)	37	2	39
18.	Technical Worker (skilled and semi - skilled)	53	nil	53
19.	Medical Practitioner (having diploma and licence to practice)	2	nil	2
20.	Carpenter	8	nil	8
21.	Shoe-maker	1	nil	1
22.	Plumber	1	nil	1
23.	Embroidery Worker	nil	1	1
24.	Mason	3	nil	3
25.	Welder	3	nil	3
26.	Gardener	2	nil	2
27.	Fitter	4	nil	4
28.	Goldsmith	1	nil	1
29.	Turner	1	nil	1
30.	Tailor	6	1	7
31.	Driver (bus and private car)	18	nil	18

| 32. | Nurse | .. | .. | nil | 1 | 1 |
| 33. | Decorator | .. | .. | .. | 1 | nil | 1 |

---

* In addition to the 400 respondents as many as 59 members of their households responded to our questions on occupation. This led to the increase in the total number here.

Keeping in view the variety of jobs that the slum dwellers do we would like to make the following observations :

A slum dweller is not merely a slum dweller but essentially a worker whose services are needed by the city and that the slums are the residential localities of the working class. Those who are self-employed and unemployed, they too are parts of the working class in the city. That this category of the working class is distanced and appear separated from the organised working class employed in the factories, is a different issue which would need separate explanation. What is significant for us here is to recognise that the slums of the city have a working class character lending them a specificity.

Further, the stereotype image of a slum dweller as a lazy, inferior, unintelligent and degraded being, resigned to his fate and lacking in motivation and thus living in a 'culture of poverty' is a jaundiced view at one level and one of contempt and dismissal at the other. The data relating to the slum dwellers' occupations presented above and our experience and encounter with them and the members of their families during the field work suggest that they are ready to change, take up challenge, strive and struggle with a generally hostile city environment. They appear to have adjusted their life styles to the various kinds of disadvantages and deprivations. An outsider tends to view this as an indication of their attitude to life, an attitude marked by a sense of servility, loss of hope and resignation to fate. However, a close examination and understanding of the way these slum dwellers fight against the odds in their everyday existence would dispel this view. That they too are capable of rising spontaneously and participating in mass action against authorities is clearly visible when threatened with evictions and demolitions. A slum dweller is a live and dynamic being as any other category of city dweller is.

Thirdly, the slum habitat is the best possible and a very rational choice in the circumstances of the slum dweller. He leaves his village/his native place in search of employment and a better life. His new home, the slum, represents an improvement over his earlier residence and existence. Over a period of time he is able to make a convenient link between his new residence and his new workplace. He is able to shape his relationship to the slum he lives in. He starts participating in the different activities of the slum and creates there a new social world for himself. He constantly strives to improve his economic position and demonstrates his mental readiness to bring improvements in the physical surroundings the moment he has an opportunity. He has practically nothing left to better his housing condition and even then he tries his best to do that at the first available opportunity.

These are some of the facts which any study of slums and slum dwellers must be informed with. We proceed below to have a look at the income structure of the slum dwellers in our sample.

Income. Over three-fourths of the total number of respondents were found to be earning less than Rs. 400/- (Rupees four hundred) a month. Among them there were forty-one persons who stated that their monthly income did not go beyond Rs. 100/- (Rupees one hundred) a month on an average, ninety-five said they were earning less than Rs. 200/- (Rupees two hundred) a month, for a hundred of them it was Rs. 300/- (Rupees three hundred) and less a month, and for the rest one hundred and nineteen of them it was Rs. 400/- (Rupees four hundred) and below a month.

As the table (see Appendix) would show, in the income brackets described above there are forty-nine of the total fifty-one women respondents in our sample. The figures suggest that lower the income of the male members of the family, higher the rate of participation of the women members in the family towards income generation. In such households where the heads of the family are not able to earn enough for physical survival, women in the family have to go out in search of work. Whether they like it or not is besides the point here. In several cases, grown-up children are also made to participate in wage earning activity

Nearly 14 per cent of the slum dwellers in our sample stated that their monthly income ranged between four hundred (Rs. 400/-) and five hundred (Rs. 500/-) rupees. In this income bracket there was only one woman respondent. About four per cent (4%) said that they earned every month over Rs. 500/- (Rupees five hundred) and above but not exceeding Rs. 600/- (Rupees six hundred). Here also there was one woman respondent.

There were eight persons who showed their monthly income ranging between rupees six hundred and seven hundred (Rs. 600-700/-). For six persons it was above Rs. 700/- (Rupees seven hundred) but less than Rs. 800/- (Rupees eight hundred). In the income brackets of Rs. 800-900/- (Rupees eight hundred-nine hundred) and Rs. 900-1000/- (Rupees nine hundred-one thousand) there were six persons, three in each bracket. Two respondents told us that they had a monthly income of Rs. 1000/- (Rupees one thousand) and above, the maximum being Rs. 1250/- (Rupees twelve hundred and fifty) on an average in the case of a shop-keeper resident of the colony. In none of these income brackets described here there was any woman respondent.

A statistical computation of data on income and occupational status (see the relevant table in Appendix) suggests that these two are interdependent. Skilled workers and the self-employed are able to earn much more than the unskilled ones.

On an average the monthly income of a skilled worker was found to be approximately Rs. 375/- (Rupees three hundred and seventy-five). The self-employed was able to make around Rs. 337/- (Rupees three hundred and thirty seven) a month. And for an unskilled worker it was around Rs. 194/- (Rupees one hundred and ninety-four) a month.

A further computation of the data showed that on an average the monthly income per earner was around Rs. 325/- (Rupees three hundred and twenty-five) a month, slightly higher than that shown as Rs. 285/- (Rupees two hundred and eighty-five) in the 1971 census figures.

The monthly income per family was found to be around Rs. 353/- (Rupees three hundred and fifty three), quite below the figure Rs. 419/- (Rupees four hundred and nineteen), as shown in the 1971 census. Similarly, the per capita income of the slum dwellers in our sample worked out to be around Rs. 80/- (Rupees eighty) as against the 1971 census figure of Rs. 90/- (Rupees ninety).

Our data on the structure of occupation and income of slum dwellers in the city suggest two things: that they are essentially the members of the working class and that an overwhelming majority of them live below the poverty line.

What follows from these facts is that a slum needs to be treated as a workers' colony and not as a place where 'marginals', 'unwanted' and the 'refuse' of the village first and the city now, live. The slum dwellers are part and parcel of the city's working class, and the city owes its existence to the labour and the various kinds of services provided by them.

PHYSICAL ENVIRONMENT, FOOD AND HEALTH

We made an enquiy in some detail regarding the conditions of living in the slums in our sample. We also asked our respondents to tell us about the kind of food they and their family members generally took. And then we asked them some questions pertaining to their health. We present here the picture that emerges from this enquiry.

Physical Condition of Living

It is a part of our general knowledge that the slums in the city, almost invariably, are very much deficient in basic civic amenities particularly with respect to water supply and lavatories. Before we launched our field study we thought conditions in these four slums, since they come in the category of relocated and improved type, would not be that appalling. But a general survey of these slums showed that for the majority of slum dwellers here also there did not exist any basic amenities like water supply and toilet facilities. Even where such facilities existed the number of users per tap or toilet was unimaginably high in several cases. This suggests that the amenities to be provided under the Slum Improvement Board Act of 1973 has remained largely as yet another piece of legislation not to be considered seriously for implementation. This, however, is not to deny the existence of a few latrines and some water taps provided by the municipal authorities in these areas where thousands of human beings live. And a few water taps, as we were informed by the slum dwellers, came to the area only after the palm of authorities were adequately greased.

If one works out the ratio between the number of users and the water tap/latrine available in these areas, an abysmal picture emerges. On an average the number of users per tap is about 800 (eight hundred) people. In Maya Nagar slum the situation is slightly better as compared to Bharat Nagar, Golibar colony and Hanuman Tekdi.

The entire Golibar slum which includes Hanuman Tedki was studied in 1968-69.[*] This study found out that Golibar colony (also called Society) had 20 (twenty) water taps and Hanuman Tekdi had 14 (fourteen) taps. These figures included only two public taps, one of them being in a lavatory block constructed by the Municipal Corporation. The remaining taps were the private property of a few 'landlords' of the area and certain groups of households. Such tap owners sold water to the people of the area. Selling water is a brisk business in the slums of Bombay.

We went to this area for our study in 1978, nearly nine years after the first study. We found that during this period only two additional water taps were installed by the Municipal Corporation in the area—one in Golibar colony and one in Hanuman Tekdi. As the population of the area increased during the period the situation had become much worse. In some pockets of this area the number of users per tap was nearly one thousand people. In effect it meant having no water tap at all. Private tap owners in both categories had increased the rate of sale from Rs. 3-5 (Rupees three to five) to Rs. 8-10 (Rupees eight to ten) per pot per month.

The water situation did not appear any better in Bharat Nagar. People living at the outskirts of this slum, and they number in thousands, used ditch water for bathing, washing clothes and other such purposes except drinking. Drinking water was bought everyday from the owners of the private taps in the interior of the slum. These people do not come in the category of the resettled slum dwellers. They have 'encroached' upon the area by paying money to the slum 'lords' operating in

*See Desai, A.R. and S.D. Pillai, "A Profile of an Indian Slum" (1972).

the locality. Several families in this slum as in Hanuman Tekdi were found using water from lavatory taps Water is such a dearly available commodity for the slum dwellers in the city.

The situation regarding lavatories in the four slums under survey appeared to be much worse. Hanuman Tekdi and large part of Bharat Nagar were in the worst condition. There were only two latrines in Hanuman Tekdi and not a single one in those parts of Bharat Nagar where 'unauthorised' hutments are located—the eastern and northern parts of this slum. It was difficult for us to count the number of hutments and the dwellers in these parts of Bharat Nagar. But by any reckoning the number of the dwellers there must run into at least four-five thousand. For these people as for several thousand other residents in these areas, the open space around was the only place where they could go to attend to nature's call. The western portion of Bharat Nagar where authorities have built 'pacca' chawls for sweepers and scavangers evicted from Kherwadi there were some lavatories. These lavatories looked dilapidated and extremely dirty. As this area is a low-level area it abounds in ponds appearing to be perennial. Such perennial ponds, the latrines, the place of bathing, washing clothes etc. appeared to be one and the same place for them. The large number of pigs roaming around had turned the area into a wretched place beyond imagination.

As compared to the situation obtaining in the areas described above, the condition regarding toilet facilities in the interior of Bharat Nagar, in Golibar society, some parts of Hanuman Tekdi and Maya Nagar, appeared to be less miserable. In these areas an average estimate of the users per latrine would work out to over 1000 (one thousand) persons. This means that they like those living in slums without any toilet facilities, use open space whenever possible. Lack of these facilities causes untold miseries to the slum dwellers, particularly to their women folk. They can attend to nature's call in open space only in the dark hours before dawn and after sunset. Our lady investigator came to know of a case in Maya Nagar where one evening 'goondas' lifted a young girl from the open space and raped her. She had gone there to attend to the nature's call.

So far as the amenities like street lights, drainage and pathways are concerned, these were virtually absent in all the four slums. With the result that when one moves in these areas after sunset one has to struggle hard to locate the lanes and by-lanes to reach his destination. Hutments are so over-crowded and built one upon another that for a new comer it is almost impossible to move easily in most of the areas in these slums. These huts have hardly any space in between them resulting in extremely narrow pathways, and these pathways are littered with kitchen rubbish, faeces of infants, and discarded materials. It is almost impossible to locate a place in these slums that is not narrow, damp and dirty. The physical condition of these areas worsens with the arrival of monsoon.

Food

We compute below the data available on the consumption of such food items by our respondents that are considered to be of high nutritional value :

Break-up of Food Items

Items	Take often (%)	Seldom (%)	Never (%)
1. Vegetables	61	38	1
2. Fruits	5	45	50
3. Milk	35	28	37
4. Eggs	4	41	55
5. Meat	14	59	27
6. Fish	28	43	29

This break-up of food items was assumed as valid for children also, since it has been observed that children do not have any special food routine in slum households as different from those of the adults.

As evident, the basic requirements of protein and calorie needs are mostly met with through a high consumption of wheat, rice, 'dal' and vegetables. Their low income does not permit them to have milk, eggs, fruits etc., regularly. No accurate measures of the nutritional level of the slum dwellers could be estimated as such a survey would require a particular kind of expertise and enough time.

It can safely be generalised that nutrition level is closely linked with the level of income. Roughly, for an average-sized family as found in this study, the required minimum income should be Rs. 400/- (Rupees four hundred) per month (for food alone) to have a balanced diet. Our respondents, as the vast bulk of the population in the country, earn much less than this amount to afford a balanced diet. Therefore, the question of high nutritional value food for them does not arise at all.

The worst affected of this situation in our sample slums appeared to be the children below the age of twelve. It was evident that most of them suffered from malnutrition.

Health

Different studies of slums throughout the world have shown that slum areas have higher incidence of infant mortality, disease and illness. Low level of literacy, low income resulting in under-nutrition and malnutrition, lack of cleanliness and the physical surroundings unworthy of human living combine to lead to a very sad state of health in slums.

All this is corroborated by the enquiry made in our sample slums regarding the state of health of the slum dwellers there. We have seen that conditions relating to water supply and lavatory facilities are awful in these areas. Either there is no system of drainage or if initially there was any, it does not function now. In absence of any proper cesspool kitchen wash, watery filth and all other liquid waste including excreta get accumulated just outside the huts and remain there for a long period of time, almost throughout the year. And each monsoon brings with it a fresh load of miseries for the slum dwellers. Dirt and filth from all surrounding areas is drained on to these slums. Breeding of mosquitoes, flies and other insects continues unabated. There is absolutely no provision made either by the municipal authorities or by the residents of the area for keeping the locality even tolerably clean. Slum dwellers appear as part of such foul atmosphere. Structure and arrangement of huts leave no room for any fresh air and natural light. And in each tiny hovel at least five to six persons on an average sleep and rest. This was the situation when we did our survey work.

Data collected from sample huts on disease and treatment showed that the residents suffered from various types of illness and, if they went at all, they went for different kinds of treatment like Allopathy, Ayurvedic or Unani, Homeopathic and household remedies (listed in the table in Appendix as village treatment). We compute below the answers of the respondents :

Thirty-six per cent reported that they had one or the other illness. Seventy-nine per cent of them preferred Allopathy; for 12 per cent of them it was household remedies on which they largely depended; for another 6 per cent Ayurvedic including Unani, and to the rest 3 per cent Homeopathy provided the cure.

Twelve per cent reported that they suffered from T.B. Little over three·fourths of them said that they were taking treatment from medical doctors (Allopathic). The remaining responsidents were actually without any proper medical attention.

Twelve per cent suffered from rheumatism, and 16 per cent from cough, cold, fever etc. as they reported. Whether they also were advancing towards tuberculosis or they already had it, we kept wondering. For we know that for the poor and the ignorant tuberculosis, especially during the early stages, passes on for 'severe cough'.

The other predominant types of illness reported were jaundice, 'stomach trouble' (meaning chronic dysentery and diarrhoea), asthma, typhoid, etc. Physicians of any variety were consulted by our respondents only when they thought that it was a case of emergency.

Our observation is that these slum dwellers have health needs. They do not have health demands. Medical treatment has emerged in our society as a commodity being sold and bought in the market. And there are good and not-so-good varieties of medical treatment available in the market. It depends on one's purchasing power, the financial capacity, that one is able to buy the kind of medical treatment, available. Then there is another factor that also needs to be taken into account—health consciousness. The slum dwellers and the poor in general are doubly disadvantaged. On the one hand they have very little capacity to pay (if at all they have) and on the other their consciousness to health is at a very low ebb.

The role of public hospitals in the city in terms of providing medical attention to the slum dwellers is at best marginal. 'Who cares for the poor there', 'Unless somebody knows you there, you do not get any treatment', 'Hospitals are far away, commuting everyday is not possible', 'Medicines given there are nothing but red-water' were the answers given by our respondents when asked about their 'visit/no visit' to the hospitals in the city.

Doctors, Vaidyas, Hakims and Homeopaths these slum dwellers go to have their dispensaries located mostly around the area. Some of them have their dispensaries situated within the slum areas. Such dispensaries have semi-permanent structures of zinc sheets and hardly looks a doctor's place. Those situated outside the slum areas proper, appear in a better shape.

As we were informed such medicine men, particularly medical doctors have 'very good' business. The slum dwellers go to them till they are able to sustain the drug imposed by the medical profession on the ailing. Capacity to sustain such drug comes to an end soon and then visits to quacks and other healers begin. Trial is given to home remedies also in between. This seemed to be the general situation with regard to illness and treatment in our sample slums.

EVICTION

I

Slum dwellers in Bombay live under the shadow of a constant threat of eviction and demolition of their huts. It can happen anytime. Newspapers carry, regularly, stories of demolitions and ensuing violence inflicted on slum dwellers by the police and the 'demolition squads' formed by the Bombay Municipal Corporation. The tempo and the intensity of eviction and demolition of slum colonies have increased considerably since the passing of the Maharashtra Vacant Lands Act of 1976—empowering the relevant authorities with unusual and extreme powers to evict people from the so-called 'vacant lands'. Evacuated people are either asked to leave the city or accommodated very far away from the central areas of the city. Those who are driven soon take shelter somewhere else awaiting another eviction and demolition. Those who are relocated in far-off areas for them there is often a total dislocation in terms of their settlement. Persons with regular employment in central areas are now forced to travel long distances for work. Those who are self-employed like hawkers, petty shop-keepers, vendors, cobblers, carpenters etc., lose their clientele built up by them over a period of time in the areas of their former residence and face untold miseries in terms of livelihood. For them it means total uprooting not only at emotional level but also at economic level.

Our report carries some case studies of such evictions and demolitions brought out by some local newspapers. We have arranged them separately in the last chapter of this report.

II

As pointed out earlier Bharat Nagar, one of our sample slums, inhabits people evicted from Kherwadi. We contacted 140 of them and administered a structured questionnaire to know their present status and reactions. Before we describe their answers, we would like to point out that this category of evicted people does not really represent the vast bulk of the evicted slum dwellers in Bombay. Those who lived in Kherwadi had a kind of special treatment in the sense that their new residential place was not very far from their former residence; they were informed quite in advance that they would be shifted to a new place; people belonging to the scheduled castes and other minority community were given a number of promises like provision of 'pucca' dwelling structures, civic facilities, pathways etc., some of which were fulfilled also. Influential politicians who had built a 'useful' network for themselves in the colony were there to 'safeguard' the interests of their slum dweller-voters. Thus, by and large, these people did not have a bad deal. The story of the majority of evicted and demolished slums in the city has been very different. We get a glimpse of the status and reactions of such slum dwellers in the last chapter of our report. We have included these newspaper reports to supplement our data on eviction.

III

We describe below the answers of our respondents pertaining to the questions on eviction. (For questions, see the relevant tables in Appendix).

Ninety-four per cent said they had the rent receipts, 59 per cent had the photopass, and *90 per cent of them (holding photopass) did not know that owning a photopass would not make them permanent.* Ten per cent of the rest (holding photopass) reported that they were misinformed by the local authorities that a photopass would make them permanent. Ninety per cent did not know of the

Vacant Land Act as such. They only knew a bit here and there. Sixty per cent felt that slums were temporary.

Majority of the respondents knew that the notice period for demolition was 30 days, the courts were powerless to prevent demolition, armed police could be used for demolition, the police atrocities could not be questioned in court etc.

Most of them did not know that the money they paid was not rent but 'a fine', and that part of the money they paid would be used for their own eviction etc.

Ninety per cent said that they did not want to pay the 'rent' (or fine) because they had no money. All of them kept mum on the question relating to giving bribes to the local authorities.

Number of them knew that the eviction was carried out on some pretext, like improvement, construction of new roads, widening of the roads, construction of sanitary blocks etc. Fifty-six per cent said that they did not want to move to the suggested (new) place. Most of them saw no justification in the reasons put forward by the Government for eviction. Most of them were given notice in writing and a few of them were orally informed of the eviction. Ninety-seven per cent said that the attitude of the police was quite unfavourable during eviction. The police had even abused the women-folk. A few complained of the unfavourable attitude of the Tehsildar, Bill Collector etc.

Eighteen persons said that they had given money to the authorities for their eviction (not as bribe). Sixteen persons gave more than Rs. 100/- each. All of them received the receipts for the money they had paid.

Large number of the respondents said they did not oppose the eviction. Presumably they knew that it was fruitless and that after all the new place was not going to be very far from Kherwadi. Promises were also made to make the new place of residence more attractive. There were some who opposed the eviction by organising a 'morcha'. Some of them informed the investigators that important people bribed them to seek their support in favour of eviction.

Sixty-five per cent of the evicted persons felt that the relocated area (Bharat Nagar) was *worse* in regard to the public facilities and services like water supply, W.C.s; nearness to work place, schools, hospitals, post office; availability of electricity; co-operation from neighbours; and in regard to the safety of women. For nearly one-fourth of the respondents these facilities were not better in their former residence. For nearly one-tenth this new place was slightly better.

FIELD-STUDY

(B) A PROFILE OF SLUM WOMEN

During the course of this field study of the 'relocation and improvement of slums in the metropolis of Bombay' certain striking features emerged. It was noted that in the areas under study— Bharat Nagar, Hanuman Tekdi, Golibar Colony, Maya Nagar— a large number of women were engaged in gainful employment other than their own household work. It was found that the slum women in Bombay enjoy a sense of freedom in terms of their movements outside their home also. It was, therefore, realised that a separate study by itself is a must to know more about women in Bombay slums.

As a preliminary step one hundred married women were interviewed from the above mentioned slum areas randomly. An interview schedule was used for the purpose. Attempts were made to record their feelings on the general slum environment, the degree of tension, fear and exploitation to which they are frequently subjected to, the role they play in the household matters, their status in the society they live, and the degree of equity in the husband-wife relations etc. Since we have interviewed only a hundred, we have used percentage only where it was essential and the rest of the places we have recorded the numbers. (Relevant tables are put in Appendix).

I

Majority of them were Hindus (52). Muslims (18) formed a minority. Neo-Buddhists (30) constituted a sizeable chunk. Neo-

Buddhists did not appear enthusiastic to speak about their castes. 28 of the total sample said they belonged to the scheduled castes, 11 of them said they were from the backward classes and the remaining 43 chose to keep silent.

When asked about the occupation of their parents only 49 of them responded. The enquiry reveals that their parents were farmers (13) tilling their own land, landless labourers (17), factory workers (9) and handicraft workers (1). Very few were in business (3) and in whitecollar jobs (4). Only 2 of them did sundry jobs to maintain their family. 16 of these women reported that they had to work hard during their childhood to help the family.

Response on literacy and education was also poor. Only 59 answered to the question on literacy and education. 10 out of these 59 never had any schooling. 5 of these were able to learn how to read and also to write 'any how' after their marriage. Of course this knowledge was confined only to their own language. 7 of them were illiterate. 22 went up to the primary level, 21 up to the upper primary level and 1 left the high school before completing the examination. 3 women had completed successfully the secondary school certificate examination and 2 were graduates with B.A. degree. We also had some questions for them on their reading habits. Of the total 50 literate and educated, 19 claimed that they read 'books' regularly. What kind of books?—mostly cheaply priced paperback novels. 9 women said that they read language dailies regularly and six said they were interested in reading magazines. 4 of them could not specify their reading materials but claimed to be interested in reading 'something' almost every day. 12 women said they did not have time to read and were not particular about it. An interesting picture emerges from this enquiry—nearly fifty per cent of the slum women appear to be literate and nearly forty per cent of them seem to have an awareness of the significance of regular reading. This kind of generalization will always be questioned because of the very limited sample size and also the authenticity of the answers given. However this picture should encourage a detailed enquiry into the literacy level of the slum women particularly in the context of our general impression that women in slums are illiterate and far from the culture of the literate.

How did they come to live here in these slums? 35 of them shifted to this slum after their marriage. 23 of them were dissatisfied with the old place (slum) they lived in and 'managed' to move to the present place of their residence. 16 women faced acute accommodation problem in the place of their earlier residence and 'succeeded' in moving to their present place of residence. 14 of them said that 'they' were unemployed before moving to their present place and it was during the search for jobs that they visited the place of their present residence and 'decided' to live there. One of them said that her family had to move to the present place because of the harassment by a slum 'dada' there—the place of earlier residence. 11 women did not respond to the question. Thus, besides migration from outside the city there is enough inside migration within the city leading to the growth of slums. This is not a new finding. This enquiry only confirms such findings.

II

An attempt was made to have a general idea about the family life of these 100 women in the sample of the study. Questions on age at marriage, dowry, husband-wife relationships, children, family planning etc. were asked. Their response to such questions is computed below :

The average age at the time of marriage of a slum woman was 13.3 years. 50 of them were married off when they were in the age group of 11 to 15 years and 35 got married when they were between 16 and 25 years of age. 15 women did not answer this question. Perhaps they were not very sure about their age at the time of marriage. But this is only a guess.

Nearly one-fourth of them reported that their parents had to give dowry at the time of marriage. For the remaining three-fourth of the respondents dowry was not a question in marriage. 19 out of 24 who said that payment of dowry was required, also specified the amount. If one calculates the figures, the average amount of dowry paid by a woman's family was around rupees Two Thousand Thirteen, and nearly fifty per cent of them (women's parents) had to borrow money from private sources on interest rates ranging from ten per cent to forty per cent. Interesting thing to take note of is that for the majority of them the system of dowry did not exist in practice.

Of the 100 women, 67 lived with their husbands. 3 were divorced, 6 widowed and 1 separated from her husband. 23 of them chose to keep silent. This category of the respondents appears rather intriguing. Did they live separately, estranged from their husbands? Did they have men other than their husbands with whom they shared life? It is difficult to say. Unfortunately this question was not probed further as they showed positive disinclination to discuss the matter any further. Discussing one's sex life with an outsider is not only undesirable but also an unpleasant act for most of us. It is more so with women. Only 2 of the 10 separated, divorced and widowed said that they were planning to remarry.

'Has your husband any other woman/women besides you?' was a question which evoked positive answer from only 7 out of 100 in the sample. 5 of them said 'yes' and 2 said 'no'. 93 of them did not respond. By inference one can say that either they were not sure about their husbands' extra-marital sex life or they knew that they had such relationships outside but did not want to reveal it to a stranger.

That the slums under investigation had prostitutes living there was revealed by 77 of the total respondents. They, however, did not want to talk about the involvement of the men around with these prostitutes. But they had some opinion on the reasons why women take to prostitution. For example, majority (54) of them thought that the 'desire' to earn more money take women to the world of prostitution. Poverty (16), compulsions (3) by 'bad' men around, and 'mere fun' (3) were other reasons behind prostitution according to them. Only one of them said that illiteracy was the reason. 23 women did not have any answers to this question.

'Is there a fight between them and their husbands?' 'What are the causes leading to fights?' For nearly fifty per cent (48 'do not fight', 1 no response) of them 'house was peaceful', 'no major quarrels', 'no fights'. 17 of them said that occasionally there were quarrels with their husbands mostly over money matters (14). 1 of these 17 women reported that because of in-laws (husband's parents) there were occasional fights and 2 said that their husbands' hot temper was the cause of occasional fights. For 34 of them home was far from being a peaceful place for there was always a fight between them and their husbands and reasons being money (10), excessive drinking (13), other women (3), inlaws (3), and any minor issues (4). 1 of these 34 stated that her husband did not like her and, therefore, there were regular fights between them. When asked about their husbands' drinking habits 87 of them said that their husbands did not drink. What probably they meant by this was that they were not habitual drunkards. The other 13 said that their husbands indulged in excessive drinking and 'always' came home drunk.

Some questions were asked on the number of children they had, their schooling, family planning practice etc. Their answers indicate that in these slums on an average a woman had 3.5 children out of which 2 were males. Only 17 of the total respondents wanted to have additional children. The rest were happy and satisfied with the number of children they had. 14 of the 17 in the above category wanted to have one more child. Of the remaining three, 2 wanted to have two more children and 1 three more. What was their awareness to family planning? Did they practice it in the past? Were they practising it now? 86 of the total sample responded to these questions. 33 of them practised it in the past. 10 of these 33 stopped practising it after some time, but the remaining 23 continued practising it. The remaining 51 of the 86 who responded said that they knew about family planning and its utility, but did not want to practice it. Unfortunately, this survey did not probe further to know the causes of not practising it. That would have given us some idea about the social, economic or cultural hurdles before the practice of family planning.

An attempt was made to measure their awareness of the medical facilities available and its use by them. Where did they deliver their children and who attended them at the time of delivery? 59 of the total sample reported that at the time of delivery they went to the municipal hospital nearby. 1 said that as she could not go to the hospital at the time of delivery a doctor was called at home. 14 of them had qualified midwife attending on them at home during delivery. 10 were helped by local 'dhais' at that time. 16 did not respond to the questions. Here again this survey failed to probe further. What happened to them? Do they not have any child or was there any miscarriage? This number appears constant here which gives the impression that they were childless. But this is only a conjecture.

67 of them answered affirmatively when asked about any special diet available to them during pregnancy. Only 2 said that they continued throughout with their usual routine food. The remaining 65, according to their answers, had special kind of diet towards the advanced stage of pregnancy. 31 did not respond.

As large number of these women were on jobs outside they were asked to specify the place where they kept their minor children when they moved out for work. Of the 52 who responded to this question 6 left their children in the school, one in her friend's place, two in their in-laws place and 43 left their children at home. None of them said that they knew about any creches around.

Very few of the children belonging to the women in this sample go to school. 67 women in the total sample said that their children did not go to school. Only 17 of them said that their children went to a school. 16 did not respond. What happens to the large number of children if they really do not go to any school. Do they go for any work? Do they loiter around while their parents are away from home? If we compare this figure with the literacy figure of the slum women, the result appears rather intriguing. Unfortunately, this preliminary enquiry did not go further into this question.

Child beating appeared to be a common phenomenon in the slums under investigation. 64 of the respondents said without any hesitation that they beat their children frequently. It was 'necessary' to keep them on the 'right path'. Twenty of them beat their child 'rarely'. Sixteen did not respond.

The world of slum children suggests as not only a fascinating but an urgent area of research and investigation. How does the social milieu around shape the personality of a slum child? How does he/she grow to become an adult person? What kind of attitudes he/she tends to develop towards the world outside his/her place of residence and existence? A host of other such questions can be raised and answered through research.

III

This survey had some questions on women's views on matters like work at home and outside, family planning, children's care and education and so on. An attempt was made to ascertain their views on matters particularly in the context of men's roles vis-a-vis theirs. Their answers are computed below and the percentages shown in brackets :

1. Women should look after home (82%).
2. Men should do house-work (59%).
3. House-work is not boring (82%).

4. House-work is not too heavy (81%).
5. All women should have children (95%).
6. Men should also care for children (85%).
7. Only a mother can look after a child (82%).
8. Women should spend full time on children (71%).
9. A child would not develop fully if he/she is with the mother all the time (40%).
10. If men earn enough, women need not go for work (67%).
11. Women should also work because it would make her independent (24%).
12. Women should have equal rights as men (82%).
13. Women's first duty is towards household work (86%).
14. Women should get equal wages as men (64%).
15. Women can work very well like men (85%).
16. Education is a must for male as well as female children (96%).
17. Men are more privileged (91%).
18. A wife must obey her husband (69%).
19. There should be no dowry system (68%).
20. Family Planning is good (93%) and everybody should practice it.
21. There should be a boy in every family (87%).
22. There is nothing wrong in abortion (58%).
23. Abortion should be made free in Bombay (73%).

It was interesting to hear women speak their mind on matters which relate to their status in society and also the self-perception of their roles vis-a-vis those of men as life-partners. Looking at their views on the above mentioned issues, should we call them as 'backward' or quite 'enlightened' in the sense that these terms are are used in common parlance? How would they compare with women of upper middle class homes or for that matter with upper class homes in respect to their views on these matters? No categorical answer on these women being quite 'enlightened' or 'backward' can be given on the basis of this study for various methodological reasons. But one thing can perhaps be said safely that the stereotypes we have of slum women in the minds of common city dwellers are not correct. And yet several assumptions of intellectuals who read and write on our city life seem to be based on such stereotypes. Such assumptions need corrections.

Their response to the question on decision-making on issues like number of children they should have, household budget, children's marriage, their schooling etc., were also revealing. Here there were only 3 women who did not respond. The rest 97 responded freely. Forty-nine per cent said that all decisions regarding household matters like family budget, children's marriage, their schooling etc., were taken after consulting each other. For thirty-two per cent of them it was mainly the husband's prerogative so to say while for nineteen per cent of them it was their (women's) prerogative.

IV

What is the employment profile of these 100 women in the sample of this study? As their response to the question revealed, on an average these women spent four and a half to five hours daily on household chores like cleaning, cooking, child care and miscellaneous work. For some women their young children came to help or were made to help them. Their men seldom helped them in household work.

Besides 11 of them from whom there was no response 56 were gainfully employed outside and 33 did not have any job at the time of interview. These 33 were employed earlier mostly as domestic maids and were now in search of 'suitable' work. Preference was always for a 'factory' work as there was more money in that kind of job and also several other benefits and privileges never available in domestic employment. Out of 56 employed 40 (nearly seventy-one per cent) had jobs as maidservants and only 9 (nearly sixteen per cent) were employed in factories.

One of the 56 said that she was given work to do on piece basis which she did at home. Six others of the total employed did sundry jobs outside home. For nearly 88 per cent of them their job meant daily work without any break and it ranged from 5 to 8 hours a day. Those who worked as domestic hands there was no question of maternity leave or medical facility and such privileges which go with a factory job. Even those who worked in factory did not enjoy these privileges uniformly. Accurate data on their monthly wages could not be obtained. An idea about it, however, can be obtained from the relevant table on 'distribution of women by present wage x first wage from the present job.' Raise in their income from the wage over a period of time was negligible. Sixty per cent of them said that their income remained more or less fixed and there was virtually no rise in it.

The respondents were asked to specify the property, if any, owned by them/their family. Thirty of them reported that their family owned 'some' land in their native place. Fifty per cent in this category also said that there was no yield from their land. For the remaining half income from land was meagre and hardly available to them. 'Relatives' living there consumed whatever was produced. Thirty-one of the women interviewed owned some jewellery in terms of gold and silver. How much gold and how much silver? None of them were specific and they tried to avoid this question. Seventeen of them owned house in their native place. House probably meant here a pucca residential accommodation and not a hut of any kind. Eight of them had small 'shops' in the locality run by the family and the only source of their earning. Four of the total sample stated that they did not have any property.

The picture given above does not really enlighten us on the economic condition of these slum women in a specific manner. That they constitute the category of the urban poor is obvious and self-evident. Only one important fact that emerges from this study is that a majority of the slum women appear to have their own distinct personality as working partner and breadwinner of their family, and that no study of urban poverty or enquiry into the economic structure of slum family can be complete without identifying the role of women as breadwinner for the family.

When asked about the amenities available to them in the area of their residence they complained that the 'government' treated them as 'animals'. Ninety-five out of 100 said that they did not have even the minimum water supply facilities. According to their answers in Bharat Nagar and Hanuman Tekdi one water tap was there to serve the needs of as many as three hundred families. Several of them narrated their everyday awful experience in indignant terms. "Where do we go for our nature call?" "Everybody, a woman at least, needs some 'pardah' for the purpose. Where is a lavatory? Who cares for us?" As their answers revealed only 10 of the 100 women had private lavatory facility. The rest 90 of them did not have any such facility and they had to 'manage' it 'any how' 'every day'. Children were allowed to defaecate and urinate 'anywhere' and 'everywhere' they managed to do it. Scarcity of water was such that it was not possible for all the members of the family to take a bath every day. Mostly the children went without proper and regular bath. At one place a particular household who had managed to have a private water connection sold water at the rate of fifty paise to one rupee per bucket. This was the experience of some of the respondents.

For 72 of them there was no supply of electricity. Out of 100 only 3 had cooking gas facility. Twenty-two of the total number did not have any ration card as they could not show their independent place of residence. Huts they lived in did not belong to them. Only 29 of them had milk cards. Buying milk regularly was not possible. 'Where is the money' was the standard answer.

Such is the world of slum women. As stated above the survey on slum women was casually done in the course of the field study just to get a glimpse of their social characteristics, their family life and their everyday existence in the area of their residence. However sketchy, we have such a picture here.

CHAPTER SIX

WRETCHED THE CITY

To supplement our data on the processes of demolition, eviction, relocation and improvement of slums in the city we reproduce below a few study reports carried out by some newspapers. Reproduction of such reports which appeared in the *Indian Express* and *Blitz* during the months of May, June and July, 1979 is verbatim. These study reports on human situation obtaining in some of the demolished, evicted, relocated and officially declared as improved slums in Bombay, provide us with such material which are not available generally in studies conducted by professional social science researchers. At least, so far as the present study is concerned, we have not come across any such study which would tell us what happens to the people affected by such programmes during and after their implementation. Any sociological study of slum relocation and improvement programmes would remain inadequate if it does not inform itself with the consequences at human level that follow the implementation of them. Reports reproduced below fill in this gap in our knowledge and understanding of human situation in slums.

We have incorporated them in the text of our study and not in Appendix as we consider them as important and relevant data on the poor in this city. Simply because the source here is newspapers, the data need not be considered as marginally important. We visited these slum areas after the publication of these reports and returned from there thinking that conditions of living could not be worse. Slum dwellers are the wretched of the city. A sense of concern, of involvement, is but natural to occur in a study of this kind which deals with questions relating to their existence in the city. These reports show such concern and involvement. So does our study. In our opinion it does not, however, make these reports less objective and, therefore, less significant.

Slums covered here in these reports are Sangam Nagar (a demolished slum without any provision of alternate accommodation), Malvani (relocated), Anand Nagar, Gavdie Pada, Vikas Nagar (all in the improved category), Indira Gandhi Nagar (relocated slum in Kandivli), chawls in and around central Bombay (a cluster of slums inhabiting scheduled castes, neo-Buddhists and Dalits), and Machimar Nagar in Mahim (a fisherman's colony in improved and developed category). Preceding these reports is a newspaper editorial which appeared in the wake of slum demolition programme undertaken by the governmental and civic authorities on an unprecedented scale in 1979. At the end of the newspaper study reports, appears a narration of eviction of Janata Colony, one of the biggest slums in Bombay, in May, 1976. The narration is based on the petition filed by the residents of the colony before the Shah Commission.

I

DEMOLISHED, EVICTED, RELOCDTED AND IMPROVED SLUMS IN THE CITY, SOME NEWSPAPERS STUDY REPORTS

A

Rehab. the Rejects

Bombay has just completed a ghoulish week of slum demolition in which thousands of slum dwellers had their wretched hutments demolished and whole families either thrown into the streets or carried by the busloads 25 miles away to the Malvani camp to be dropped like refuse into a creek of reclaimed land infested by mosquitoes, snakes and wild dogs.

All this in the name of slum clearance! We are told that nobody wants slums, that if Bombay is not cleared of the 'zopadpattis', the whole metropolis is likely to be converted into a vast stinking, plague-ridden slum.

Quite right! We cannot agree more. But hasn't it already been converted into a slum? By not only slums of the horizontal variety that are being demolished, but also of the vertical slums which are more dangerous because they can never be demolished.

Vertical Slums

What is the concrete jungle that today disfigures Nariman Point and the foreshore beyond Cuffe Parade if not a horrendous slum scraping the skies? It has all the attributes of our slum culture.

Its filth and squalor! Visit the stinking lavatories, the garbage-laden chowks, the apology for servant's quarters—and you will be sick with nausea!

Crime and prostitution? There is more of them here with smugglers, contractors, land sharks and economic offenders with a flourishing call-girl racket thrown in than at the poor, wretched hovels in which dwell the city's working men and women!

The only difference is between the horizontal and the vertical as also the wealthy and the poor.

But aren't the 'zopdis' illegal? Of course, they are—but so are most skycrapers! Just consider the towering illegality of the Bombay Stock Exchange building which has broken all rules being allowed to shoot into the sky while thousands of little hutments are being demolished!

Guilt of Government

The guilt cannot be apportioned. It lies solely and unequivocally at the Government's door. Protection of the interests of the rich and the powerful to the detriment of the poor and the weak has been the policy of the Janata no less than the Congress.

In the present case, positive action under legislative sanction to alleviate the sufferings of the slum and pavement dwellers has been withheld and scuttled at the insistence of the powerful construction lobby and its wealthy clients.

The Urban Land Act, promulgated by the Centre in 1974, was conceived and put through in order to halt speculation in land and help low-cost housing projects. Under its provisions affecting our city, no individual or company could hold land of an area greater than 500 square metres.

An exemption was made in the case of charities and projects for cheap housing; and we were assured that a massive housing programme for the poorer classes would follow the Act.

Project Scuttled

The land sharks and building contractors in collusion with a corrupt bureaucracy lost no time, however, in distorting the legislation designed to bring relief to the poor into an instrument for their exploitation. Today the builders submit fraudulent projects for low-cost housing in order to grab the land. They then sign two separate agreements with the tenants, in the second of which the price is inflated under the guise of provision of additional amenities. Thus, the object of the Act is perverted.

Under this Act, all areas which housed slums and other unauthorised construction were declared vacant land. Land so declared could not be sold without a NOC from the proper authorities. This permission is given only after an assurance that the people occupying the land—that is, the slum dwellers—would be provided accommodation on the same plot.

Vacant Land

The Government was empowered to buy any land over this limit of 500 sq. metres and also the vacant land at not more than Rs. 10 per sq. metre for the cheap housing project. The price could also be as less as Rs. 2 per sq. metre. But till today not a single yard has been taken over by a Government which claims to rule in the name of janata, the people.

The Urban Land Ceiling Act has, thus, been openly flouted by the denizens of the construction brotherhood, with the active connivance of the Government.

Direct Action

Under the earlier Land Aquisition Act, the Government was empowered to claim land, after giving compensation, for public purposes. As the slums and their improvement are part of the public responsibility of any Government, they would not be amiss if they took over land for low cost housing.

Why has the Government not assumed the responsibility of providing cheap brick-and-mortar housing for the poor? Why has the State ministry not seized land from the rich construction sharks and built on it tenements for the poor?

It is not as if the cost incurred will be phenomenal. The slum-dwellers will certainly bear a part of the expenses, in most cases, to be able to seek, shelter under a 'pucca' roof. With the monsoon clouds fast approaching, the Government should have sought to provide accommodation, instead of driving the hapless 'zopadpatti-walas' out into the city's streets.

We hold the State Government guilty of gross neglect and dereliction of duty vis-a-vis the poorest and weakest among its citizens. Their summary eviction with the demolition of the wretched hutments built by them at the cost of their blood, toil tears aggravates the guilt to a social crime.

Is there nobody—no leader, party, or organisation with a social conscience to mobilise them into a struggle for the barest necessity of a roof on their head? If the Janata has failed—their trust, then the Opposition parties must come to their rescue with a project for Direct Action.

II

WAR ON THE SLUMMERS

"Gadi Aa Gayi Hain.." the cry rises from a thousand parched throats. Far away on the horizon one could see a thin streak of police Marias, the Collectors grey vans and the trucks of the demolition squads making a beeline for the slums. We were in Sangamnagar, the site of our inaugural ward-by-ward crusade. It is now its turn to bite the dust for the homes of countless slum-dwellers will, in a short while, be torn apart.

With a pincer movement, the trucks have entirely surrounded the area. The atmosphere is electric and tense. The slum-dwellers have made a makeshift line in front of their huts. The situation could take an ugly turn, but their leaders have urged them to exercise restraint. There were attempts by the Cuffe Parade residents to halt demolition. They realise that resistance is hopeless.

It was a dog day afternoon, with the sun mercilessly beating lown on the seared earth. The profusion of indigo and khaki-clothed policemen are watched with a mixture of bewilderment and awe. Some of them have rifles and tear gas shells. The show of force is supposed to cow the populace and prevent a repetition of Cuffe Parade. It did succeed in aborting any violence, but it left a bad taste in the mouth. The corrupt police had assumed the role of an oppressor.

Government Assailed

The Collector, Mr. Gill, was profusely garlanded by the slum-dwellers. At a given word from their corporator, Niyaz Ahmed Vanu they start dismantling their houses. The tiles on the roof, the matting around it and the bamboo superstructure are slowly shifted. All the time there is an expectancy that perhaps the Collector would call a halt to this "home"—icide, that perhaps they could joyfully rebuild their huts.

The policy of the Government was assailed by their elected corporator. "They purposely waited until we had reclaimed the entire area before moving in. We got rubble from elsewhere in hired trucks and now they will reap the benefits."

The Collector also benignly surveyed the proceedings. The demolition squad were trying to topple a structure with the use of a stout coir rope. The method was primitive and the rope broke to a crescendo of derisive laughter. "We are demolishing this area as we consider these huts as a defence liability," said Mr. Gill. "Most of these huts are empty and are built by slum landlords. They are sold or let out for fantastic profits."

Defence Risk

This was empty justification and we are sure that in his heart of hearts, Mr. Gill realises this. That after a period of two years there should be an awakening to a defence risk sounds highly dubious. And again what about those who had paid fantastic sums to obtain residence? What about them? Mr. Gill had no coherent answer.

The demolition was on with a vengeance. The motley crew of the contractor, with red ribbons pinned on their torn undershirts as distinguishing marks, were slowly going berserk. They all seemed intent to earn their daily wage of Rs. ten.

Clusters of residents from other sectors were surrounding us. All seemed uncertain of their fate. Their faces were contorted into one question. Will our turn come tomorrow? Will we be driven on the streets without compensation? Where will we exist on the city's cruel road? For unlike the Cuffe Parade residents, the Sangamnagar slum-dwellers are not being provided alternate accommodation.

The agony and uncertainty on their faces was of one who does not know how rocky his future is going to be? We could no longer bear to be mute witnesses to a wholesale destruction of men's homes and hearths, and, thus, we quietly departed.

III

FROM CUFFE PARADE TO MALVANI

A

Plight of ejected slum-dwellers

Inside a hut made of thin straw mats in far-flung Malvani near Malad, Shanta sits on the bare floor crying softly. The tears do not stop flowing.

Three months back she was a happy woman, even though she lived in a 'zopadpatti' near Cuffe Parade. Her husband who worked in a nearby hotel earned about Rs. 300 a month. She supplemented the family income by working as a domestic help, and their only child—a four month old baby—was growing healthily.

Till one day in May when their hut was demolished by the Bombay Municipal authorities and they were flung into a reclaimed patch of open, marshy land in Malvani. Her husband had to give up his work as he was a daily wage worker, and she too could not find any employment. Then came the rains, and with it mosquitoes and diseases. They did not have the money to construct a shelter over their heads immediately. Her child got high fever and died soon after in mid-June.

Shanta's story is not a lone case. Most of the 2,000 odd

families who were dumped at New Collectors' Compound in Malvani soon after their hutments were demolished from Cuffe Parade are in the same plight today.

The land where they live is damp and marshy. The open drains which flow all round the site are breeding places for mosquitoes and flies, and sickness has invaded every family. Only one municipal dispensary serves these 8,000 people. But more than anything else the spectre which haunts them is the sudden unemployment which they are faced with.

What the civic authorities never bothered to take into consideration while razing the slum at Cuffe Parade and dumping them at Malvani was that the livelihood of these people was directly linked to the humming business and economic centre of South Bombay.

Most of them did not have regular jobs, but found casual work as labourers at nearby construction sites, in the dockyards and at shops. Many women worked in the nearby flats or found lucrative jobs at the surrounding fishing sites—cleaning prawns for example often fetched them Rs. 10 to 20 a day.

But ever since they came to Malvani, most had to give up these jobs, though a few tried to commute to town for a while. "To earn Rs. 8 to 10 a day—and that also we are not always certain of getting work—we cannot spend Rs. 5 a day". says Amir Sahib who worked as a casual labourer earlier. He has sent his wife to his village and is staying with a friend in a hut—because he has not yet been allotted a piece of land.

The best that a few manage to get are some odd jobs around. The station is a 15-minute bus ride from their site, and they are surrounded by the older slums. Their meagre savings are dwindling very fast, and very soon it may be difficult for them to manage even one square meal a day.

Take the case of Usha Male for example. She is a divorcee, and has two small children to look after. Earlier she worked at the fishing sites and managed to earn about Rs. 200 a month. Today she is desperate because she has no money—and even her neighbours point her out as one of the "really pathetic cases." "Please get me some work", she keeps on repeating—"I am ready to do anything."

The families who are slightly better off have managed to secure themselves against the rain by building stronger huts. But a

number of them did not have the finances for this, and the monsoons have wrought havoc with their temporary shelters. The
rain water seeped through, converting them into big puddles,
and in the resultant exposure to cold and dampness the inevitable
happened—many of the children fell ill.

A doctor taken by the Bombay Slum Dwellers' United Front
to this slum in late June found that malaria, broncho-pneumonia
and stomach disorders were rampant among the children.

And medical facilities being meagre, most cannot even get
adequate care. The solitary municipal dispensary manned by
one doctor obviously makes it impossible to give proper care and
attention to the hordes of patients. "When I took my child
there, the doctor told me to take him to Nanavati hospital—how
can I spend so much money reaching there?" says Abdul Rashid.
While in Cuffe Parade the dispensaries were accessible, but few
can now afford to travel everyday to the hospitals—the nearest
one being in Vile Parle.

According to the slum-dwellers, at least six children have
died ever since they shifted here—specially after the rains came.

The filth around has only helped to make the problems worse.
There is no running water and it has to be brought by tankers
every day.

Though eight bathrooms have been constructed for every
125 families, these are not being used because there is no water
and they are blocked. Instead the people use the open grounds
around, and the environmental sanitation has further deteriorated due to this.

The authorities had the site sprayed once, but the dirt and the
open drains all round make it impossible to keep away the swarms
of flies and mosquitoes, and the people complain that they cannot
even sleep at night due to this menace. There are no arrangements
for street lighting either—as no electric connection has been
provided for the lamp posts, and the entire place is submerged
in darkness after evening, attracting anti-social elements and
'goondas'.

The Chairman of the Bombay Housing Area and Development Board had reportedly promised that the people here will be
employed at a centre which they plan to open close-by to make
handicrafts and other commodities such as papads. But the pro-

ject has not taken off the ground yet, and meanwhile the people have no means of earning a living for their families.

Uprooting slums for proper urban development is all very well—but to throw them into greater misery and even snatch away their means of a livelihood surely cannot be termed as progress, say the social workers who are trying to help the people here.

Their crying need today is better living conditions, proper medical attention, and jobs and if these are not given soon, they may well sink into greater and worse misery every day.

B

HELL AT MALVANI

Even as the slum dwellers were being evicted from Cuffe Parade, Colaba, this horrifying experience was being coupled with harassment from the paid demolition squads. Side by side with the brisk 'business' of destruction of huts, the equally brisk business of issuing slips for alternate accommodation at Malvani was on.

A few hundred rupees slipped into the palms of officials making a list of names of 'refugees' who were to be shifted to the site, insured that a 15×10 sq. ft. plot at Malvani would be reserved for them.

No accommodation

More than 150 families whose huts were demolished at Cuffe Parade have not been provided with accommodation to date because they did not have the money to pay the bribe. They have been thrown at the mercy of the elements and their discomfiture has assumed gigantic proportions now that the monsoons are here.

Eleven infants between the ages of five months to two years have already lost their lives. Slum children are notoriously weak and anaemic because of their economic and social conditions and the traumatic experience of the eviction has resulted in death for some of them.

The maltreated, evicted slum dwellers have no option but to

attempt to stay on the right side of the officials. Their obsequi-
ousness has inflated the egos of Tehsildars and even the peons at
Malvani. The power that these men wield becomes immense
when one considers the importance of a roof over the head in
inclement weather.

The more vocal slum-dwellers allege that the worst culprits
are the tehsildars Nayab Shetty and Gowilkar who openly ask
for a neat sum of Rs. 50 for the allotment of a plot of Government
land. Even an ordinary chaprasi called Torne has become all-
powerful and threatens his bosses with dire consequences if
they interfere with his lucrative side-business of accepting bribes.

False pledge

The plight of the other residents of Malvani who have
managed to get a plot of land is equally bad. The Collector had
promised the slum dwellers that if they agreed to leave Cuffe
Parade they would be rehabilitated at Malvani and all basic
facilities would be kept in readiness for them.

Till today, water, electricity and sanitation remain a dream
for the Malvani 'rehavasis'. The few taps that have been provided
cannot serve even one-tenth of the Malvani population. While
toilets have been constructed they remain unused because there
is no water provided and no proper drainage system.

But now the tide has turned. The 'rehavasis' have decided
to band together and raise their voices in protest against the
raw deal that they have been doled out by the Government.

On June 5, a 30-member women's delegation of the Bombay
Slumdweller's United Front approached the Collector, seeking some relief from their travails. When their requests fell on
deaf ears, they gheraoed him and extracted a verbal assurance
from him.

They are also approaching Dr. Ishaq Jamkhanwalla and
seeking his aid in the matter. They vow that they will not rest
until at least some of their problems are solved.

C

MALVANI..PURGATORY FOR THE DISPLACED

The fifth of May had proved traumatic for the residents of the 'zopadpatti' near the World Trade Centre at Cuffe Parade. That day will be etched indelibly on their memory.

For that was when they were driven out of their homes, their hearths were trod into the ground and their huts were rent apart by the paid demolition squads of the Collector of Bombay.

They had not taken it lying down, retaliating with a little stone throwing. This, however, did not deter the squads and the protective cover of the indigo-clothed city police. There were cane-charges, tear gas and arrests. The will of the slum-dwellers was broken.

To further grind them in the dust and subjugate them, they were shifted in open lorries to Malvani, a "resettlement colony" off Malad.

The resettlement part is a bit of a joke perpetrated on the guileless slummers. They are given a bare minimum of razed land, reclaimed from the muck-infested creek. It is on this plot infested by scorpion and snake, baked earth, that the residents of Cuffe Parade were to start a fresh and new chapter in their lives.

'Forced Migrants'

It was to study the conditions firsthand and to provide an accurate reflection of the atmosphere through our pen and the cameraman's lenses that we embarked on our eleventh ward-by-ward crusade. But no superior plume or camera could truly recapture the grim desolation and hopelessness of the 'forced' immigrants.

The entire Malvani area is a vast resettlement colony, where inhabitants of all demolished slums, over the years, have been given refuge. Thus, there are people from Bandra, who have settled here for the past four years, after demolition of the old abattoir and the huts surrounding it.

The office of the Government Collector, housed in a pucca construction has a few clerks engrossed in their files. No one wishes to comment in the true spirit of Indian bureaucracy, always referring you to their immediate superior.

We can review the process of reconstruction which has commenced in full swing. The residents have adapted themselves with amazing resiliency to the alien conditions. All around us we see people at work, sawing the bamboo or fixing their thatched huts or their walls of bamboo mats.

Rehman had a flourishing business of cycle hire in the Cuffe Parade slums. At his own cost he has removed his bicycles but has no place to house them and carry on his business. All the petty traders and grain shopkeepers have been granted no premises to carry on their trade and earn their livelihood.

Poor Exploited

A lot of people seem to be making capital out of the plight of these slum dwellers. Bogus certificates are got and land is occupied. Huts are built on these plots and then either let out or sold for a fantastic profit.

The conditions out here are deplorable. There is one forlorn water pipe, jutting out of the ground and supposed to cater to two thousand people. The toilets are without doors and the tanks do not contain water.

The heat is scorching, especially in the mid-afternoons. Entire families are without a roof over their heads, and are huddled around what is left of their earthly belongings. In some cases this only amounts to a few pots and pans.

Some families have even taken refuge in concrete water pipes, with bits and pieces of sacking masking the two sides.

Mehboob Beg is another of these faceless migrants. Like most others, he was employed in the Sassoon Docks. A hand cart labourer, he used to earn Rs. five-six per day.

'Most of us are employed in the docks. We have not been able to go to work for the past five days. I have lost everything and do not have any money to start building anew.'

He, his wife and three children, were huddled around a primus stove and a few old, torn suitcases. The only scraps of food were a few morsels of stale chapati and a couple of rotten onions.

Costly Transport

The transfer has severely affected those whose livelihood was concentrated at the tip of South Bombay. Their daily travel bill, from the camp to Malad railway station, to Churchgate and by bus to Sassoon Dock costs Rs. two for a one-way journey.

Taking the return trip into consideration, a labourer earning Rs. six to ten per day has to spend over half of it in travelling.

Adjacent to the camp is the creek, infested with pestilence, from mosquitoes to scorpions. The area is also used as an open-air lavatory by the dwellers who find the constructed toilets either too far away or just stinking holes to be able to go to them.

The reclaimed land has also not been properly flattened, adding to the discomfort of those who are now sleeping under the stars and cooking in the open.

The 'zopadpattiwallas' are ultimately reconciling themselves to their fate, but their hopes and their comparatively event-free lives have been completely shattered. Their faces are unsmiling, serious, as they are now engaged in a fight to bounce back and resume normal lives.

Many Hindrances

The hindrances are considerable. All building material has to be bought once again. They have to spend over three hours commuting to work and back and spend half their earnings doing so. The terrain is unfamiliar and the Government bureaucrats have to be handled. And at what cost?

Victims of the rioting have been charge-sheeted and the entire population is collecting money for their bail. Many are lying in public hospitals with their shins broken to pieces, due to the inhuman lathi-wielding of the cops.

The Government and other authorities have completely neglected their duty of rehabilitating the displaced slum-dwellers. For rehabilitation does not mean providing only 50 sq. ft. of land. It also means granting compensation, building materials and adequate water, toilets and medical facilities. Unfortunately, none of this has been complied with and no facilities provided.

Unending Huts

The other sectors of Malvani are also one unending line of huts. Some of them are now pucca structures with one floor. But they suffer from the same predicament of less water, an even lesser number of toilets, commuting to their places of work and constantly falling prey to the scourge of disease.

The only amenity provided are Bal Kalyan Kendras, where children under the age of five are given free teaching and are taken care of during the day. This would eventually reduce the number of urchins on the street but the age limit should be further increased to include all those below the age of ten.

The resettlement colony is more like a concentration camp but without the barbed wire and the uniformed guards. For Malvani is not as bad as we thought it would be. It is much worse.

IV

'DRY LAW' AT ANAND NAGAR

A couple of miles from the Jogeshwari Station, is the sprawling Anand Nagar slum, of the 'K' ward, bearing a somnolent look, as we, from BOM-BLITZ and Arul Francis of the Bombay Slum Dwellers' United Front, approach the huts at 11 a.m. A young man peeps out of a doorway and promptly disappears. Soon the word spreads and a group of chattering hutment dwellers swarm over and offer to accompany us on our rounds.

The area is devoid of trees, bushes or any other form of vegetation. Not a drop of water is to be seen anywhere. It is in this aspect that Anand Nagar differs from the other slums that we have visited so far in our ward-by-ward crusade. Water is used extremely sparingly and there are no pools or 'nalas' of slush to be seen.

One of the men from the crowd, realising that we are pressmen, introduces himself as Prakash Phansure. Prakash is a social worker who has taken upon himself the task of improving the lot of the slum dwellers.

The plot on which the huts stand is owned by no individual or authority. The hutment dwellers are thus saved the expense of either the rent or the compensation that they would have had to pay otherwise.

"What we fail to understand", says Tukaram Kashid, President of the Anand Nagar Zopadpatti Rahavasi Sangh, "is that even though the names of each one of us was on the voting list, only 4 of the 835 huts here were numbered in the 1976 census."

Total Neglect

This colony has been totally neglected by the Corporation and by the Government. A basic amenity like water has not been granted to this vast conglomeration of huts housing more than 7,000 people.

For years the hutment dwellers pleaded with the authorities to grant them the use of at least one tap, but their appeals fell on deaf ears. Then they took it upon themselves to dig a well. Their first attempt met with failure. After three months of hard labour under the guidance of old Mohammed Yaseen, they had to abandon the fruitless task, defeated by the hard rocky layer that they came across after having dug to a depth of 12 feet.

The second attempt was a partial success. They were lucky enough to strike water at a depth of 15 feet though the flow of the water into the well was a mere trickle. This water is fit only for the washing of clothes and vessels, being hard and bitter to taste. The 'rehavasis' are forced to traverse a distance of more than two and a half miles, for their drinking water, which they obtain from a well at Behram Baug. Even this facility is available only between 7-10 a.m. and 4-5 p.m. So they are forced to depend on the local well water for drinking purposes, at times.

They bathe in a huge natural pool which is covered with some revolting green slime. Every year, at least three children fall into the slimy pool and meet their deaths by drowning.

Bath in Slime

"This scarcity of water makes our lives a misery," laments 28-year old Chandrakala, "the ill effects are visible in our children, who suffer from all the water-borne diseases from time to time." Diarrhoea and dysentery are rampant while jaundice has plagued more than half the colony to date.

It was Prakash Phansure's dynamism and force of personality that inspired the slum dwellers to stage a peaceful satyagraha near the main road fire-hydrant at Jogeshwari on May 13. More than 2,000 'rehavasis' took part in the protest rally. Their demand was very simple, the use of the water from the fire hydrant till alternative arrangements were made.

Not only was their demand rejected but hordes of them were arrested and taken away to the Andheri police station for obstructing traffic.

The members of the Anand Nagar Rehavasi Sangh are vociferous in their complaints against their corporator, Indumati Patel. They claim that their area has been totally neglected by her and that they get a glimpse of the lady only when elections are round the corner. When lakhs can be spent on the construction of a link road between Goregoan and Juhu, cannot a single tap be provided for the colony?

Dark Ages

Anand Nagar is still in the dark ages with electricity not even aspired for. Being far outside the main suburbs of Jogeshwari, the area is in pitch darkness at nightfall except for the flicker of small kerosene lamps, which very few of the slum dwellers can afford.

The Anand Nagar Mahila Aghadi has just been established. The women hope to get visitors who will impart the basics of nutrition, child-care and family-planning. Those among the women who are more educated than the rest will read out the newspapers and keep the others aware of the goings-on in the outside world.

The women in the colony bemoan the fact that there are no municipal clinics close at hand. As they cannot afford the stiff charges of private practitioners, they are forced to resort to the medicines doled out by the local quacks. The women also adopt the roles of midwives when the need arises. On the day we met them, they were very excited and voluble because one of them had delivered twins the previous evening and had almost lost her life in the process.

Illiteracy

The problem of illiteracy is also very acute here. The closest school being more than two miles away, most of the children while away their time playing under the hot sun. The only tiny school here is run by Mohammed Yasseen for children between the ages of 4 and 8. He teaches them the rudiments of the Urdu language and also imparts some religious training.

Kamal Vitthal More, who was a bright student, had her education cut short when she met with an accident on her way home from school one day. Now forced to depend on crutches to hop from place to place, she has decided to start a school for the tiny tots, with the blessings of the rest of the slum dwellers, from this June. As Jaywantibai put it, "We grew up as illiterates but envisage a better future for our children".

Although there are members of different communities living in Anand Nagar with the Harijan basti close by, there is very little communal strife .Each one is too busy, eking out a miserable existence, to harbour communal feelings.

There is only one liquor den in Anand Nagar and minor fights do arise when the 'rehavasis' are under the influence of the cheap "tharra".

Cottage Industries

A number of cottage industries have sprouted in the colony. The rest work as construction workers, stone breakers, grass cutters, etc. Gaya Prasad Yadav who came down to Bombay in 1964 has a small costume jewellery enterprise and employs four small boys to help him with his work. His income being Rs. 400 per month, he is one of the few fairly prosperous traders in the colony. Even then he cannot afford to move out.

The residents of Gavdei Pada, comprising 70-75 huts, share the problems of the Anand Nagar 'Rehavasis'. Their huts are built on the jutting rocks of the Jogeshwari creek. They are among the poorest in the colony. "We sell the small black fish that we catch in the creek and are barely rewarded with Rs. three-four at the end of a hard day's work", says one of the men, busy spreading out his net.

While the Anand Nagar residents feel fairly secure on their

tract, those of the neighbouring Vikas Nagar, are constantly under the fear of eviction. Although the huts were constructed more than 15 years ago, only 10 out of the 350 huts were numbered during the 1976 census.

The Vikas Nagar huts are constructed on the property of one Abdul Rehman of the Albani Stone Supply Company. The hutment dwellers allege that the land does not actually belong to this man but that he is hoping to grab it by greasing the right palms and pleasing the right people.

Fear of Eviction

S. Gaekwad, a resident of this slum grumbles, "We live under this perennial fear of eviction. From time to time, the henchmen of the factory-owner, descend upon our sootladen huts, to threaten us with dire consequences if we attempt to refurbish our huts." Most of the hutment dwellers are in the employ of either the Aibani Company or of the Prakash Construction Works, another big factory in that area.

"We have been demanding a fresh census survey for the past six months. Our applications were sent to the Controller of Slums but very little has been done about it," says Gaekwad. On the contrary, the harassments meted out to the slum dwellers have been intensified, and social workers like Prakash Phansure are being threatened with their very lives for activising the Vikas Nagar residents.

V

NO 'GHAR MANDIR' FOR KANDIVLI SLUMMERS

Far from the hustle-bustle of the city, in a remote corner of Bombay tucked away in Kandivli (West), stretches a vast expanse of served land. The hot, sweltering sun beats down mercilessly over this place. You look around for shelter, but all that meets your eyes are skeletal, roofless huts scattered around the place.

This is the Indira Gandhi Nagar, a place on which neither the gods nor man has showered any kindness.

We trudge deeper but the scene is unrelieved. You see some people crowded together. A strange silence hangs in the air,

pathetic faces stare at us and before you ask them a question
they break down and pour out their travails.

Hut Demolition

"All was well with us" moaned Lautram Jaiswal "but our
peace was shattered a few days back when suddenly a group of
300-400 police invaded our area, started beating us and demolishing our huts. All our belongings were confiscated and we were
left with just a few bamboos and some straw mattresses."

The incident took place at 9.30 a.m. on June 7, and continued
till the next day, when most of the men-folk of this zopadpatti
were taking out a morcha to Mantralaya to protest against the
demolition of their huts.

Only ten minutes' grace was given to vacate the place and after
this short time, there was a sudden burst of noise. Many huts
were tumbled some even burnt, people were beaten and goods
taken away. The whole area was rutted. There was shouting,
pleading, and crying, with confusion prevailing everywhere.

The reason for all this—more than 50,000 people had settled
unlawfully on a vast, dirty creek, which the Government proclaim-
ed as its own land.

"It was this dirty creek, which, due to our hard labour was
converted into a habitable place" said Solanki, one of the
residents.

The inhabitants had cut rocks from nearby areas and raised
the ground to a good four feet so that they could abide there.

Slum Rejects

Most of the people residing in the Indira Gandhi Nagar are
rejects of other 'zopadpattis'. Because no alternative accommodation was given to them all they could do was to settle on an
empty open space.

When this vast land was a waste the Government did not
bother to utilise it. For to level this creek into a habitable place
the Government would have had to spend money, which it never
does.

"Seeing the improvement after our hard work, the Government suddenly thought that this place could bring in a lot of

money if it could be sold to a private party. So to make easy money for itself, we were thrown out like a herd of cattle," said Jaiswal.

The condition is pathetic here. Many women and children are seen roaming in the hot sun, without any roof over their heads. Some are busy patching up the ruins, some just sitting idle for there is nothing left to be patched up.

What once was a busy, humming place with more than 50,000 residents now has only about 15,000 people left. All of them have run away on the sly from the torture. Those who are left behind have no relatives here and no alternative accommodation. The Government has refused to give them any compensation.

Cried out an old man with tears in his eyes "the gods have done us injustice. What have we done that we have to be punished so severely? We have never interfered in any matter. We have never troubled anyone. Oh! why this torture".

It was said by the Government that those huts which had numbers and photo-passes would not be demolished. But even such huts were razed while some of the unlicenced huts are still intact only because these residents could afford to pay the Rs. 200 demanded by the police.

Complained Baburao, a resident, "The Government makes laws but what kind of laws are these which can be altered every time a person pays some cash?"

Party Conflict

The main reason for this disruption is the inner conflict between the Janata and the Congress Party. Said Shetty one of the "strong men" of the area. "The enmity is between the parties, and it is we who have to suffer. Each party wants to show the other how powerful it is, so they ruin our place".

The residents are not bothered about the water shortage in the area and education for their children now. All that they desperately want is a roof over their heads. "When there is no 'gharmandir' (house) who wants a 'balmandir' (school)."

The situation has not changed till today. Misery still prevails. Some are lucky to have survived with a few belongings. But most of them do not even have a thing which they can claim as their own. "I have no utensils even to cook my food. Everyday I live on 'pav vadas'. The thought of how much I have to spend to rebuild my house makes me shudder. I am really miserable", wept Gauri.

The majority of the men-folk have not yet resumed their work and they are still on leave. Many of them are Government servants. There is Solanki, Arokidas Joseph from the army and many peons from Government offices. Is this the way the Government treats its employees?

Torture Inflicted

Why has so much torture been inflicted on these people? If the Government wants to remove them from the area why not does it give them alternative accommodation as the Cuffe Parade hutments were given? Many of thse people are from the villages and they do not wish to go back as things are no better there.

What was the use of beating up so many people? Couldn't the whole matter be tackled without any violence? So many people were bruised, as many as 17 huts burnt, and umpteen goods confiscated. All this harassment has created a bitter feeling and antipathy in the hearts of the people against the Government. The people here have begun to hate their political leaders.

They are all unanimous on one point. "We will stay here only and not shift. We will rebuild our broken homes, come what may, even if they break our homes again. If the Government can be ruthless, we can be even worse".

This militancy is bound to affect the State Government. This frustration and desperation of the slummers is bound to rise from a simmer and come to a boil.

VI

MONSOON CREATES 'MINI-HELL' IN RESERVED WARD

Of the five wards serving as a reserved constituency for the backward classes, ward No. 63 is one of the largest. The residents of this ward who are predominantly scheduled castes, neo-

Buddhists and Dalits are employed in the textile mills of Parel or have their own small-scale business. Many of them are vendors of spicy foodstuffs such as bhel, pani-puri, idlis and masala dosas.

Our first halt is the Abukasai Chawl opposite the Kamgar Krida Kendra, the massive stadium near the Elphinstone Mills, which was constructed at a cost of Rs. 40 lakhs. The chawl building is in an abject state of disrepair with gaping holes in the tiled roofing and dank walls almost bereft of plaster.

Some of the residents have repaired their tenements at their own cost. While those who cannot afford to do so exist in the leading shabby rooms until they are forced to leave for fear of their lives. More than 2000 people occupy these 64 tenements. The problems of water scarcity and few W.C.s pale into insignificance when one considers the problem of dangerous living quarters.

The residents had approached the BHADB for demolition and reconstruction of their building, but according to the new housing board rules, ground floor structures will neither be demolished nor reconstructed in the future. "A number of tenants have locked up their houses and left", says Ramesh Sagare, the Secretary of the RPI Bombay Pradesh.

Elite Stadium

He laments, "The corporation spent about Rs. 40 lakhs on a stadium which admits only a small section of the population, the elite, who have many more avenues of entertainment open to them. Our children are being forced to play on the streets, this area being devoid of even a single garden".

Residents have to travel long distances to fetch milk and the absence of a milk booth in this locality is badly felt. The nearest police station is the one at Dadar. There was not even a post-office close by. But with the concentrated efforts of social workers like Ramesh Sagare, Professor S. Balkrishan, etc. a mobile post office van now visits this area once a day.

As we had observed at Byculla last week, a number of huts have encroached onto the pavements outside the stadium. These are all temporary structures. The municipality is doing its best to combat this nuisance. Every few days these huts are demolished but the very next day they sprout up again. As there are no public lavatories on this stretch of road, right from the Dadar Phool Market to the Lower Parel Bridge, those who live on these pavements merely make use of the road. Most of the residents are beggars by profession.

Ambedkar Nagar, the entrance to which is wedged between the Elphinstone Mill and the stadium, consists of more than 600 shanties. The drains running along each row of huts may be conducive to the removal of dirty water and liquid effluents from each hut, but can also lead to chaos during the monsoons.

Flooded Drains

The water floods the drains until they overflow into the miserable hovels. The filth that blocks the drains is cleaned only occasionally with the result that the rubbish blocking the drains further prevents flow of rain water.

The municipality, showing rare consideration had constructed a garden for the children of Ambedkar Nagar. But all we see when we visit the garden, is a handkerchief sized plot of mud and slush. It does not resemble a garden even remotely. At one end stands a concrete hut with a window embedded in one wall.

The corporation had intended to install a TV set here for the benefit of the slum dwellers. TV programmes in Bombay being predominantly educational, it would have been of great interest to the 'rehavasis'. The only other object in the playground is a double bar, for gymnastics on which the kids frolic happily the whole day long. This double bar too was installed only after social workers insisted on it.

Illicit Brew

The police have begun taking severe action against the illicit breweries in Ambedkar Nagar. We see the police confiscating large barrels of liquor. This move was probably in anticipation of the dry days ahead, beginning from July 15.

At Ambedkar Nagar, Ramesh Sagare has established a library and a Vidhyarthi Sahayak Mandal, an organisation which will help needy and poor students. So far it has assisted more than a hundred students in geting free textbooks and notebooks.

The residents of Dholakvalla Chawl in the same Ward, are blessed with about twelve toilets. But three out of these have fallen into disuse being chock-full of filth while some of the others are bare of any kind of ceiling. Only a metal grill exists instead of a roof. These huts are built on private property but the tenants have long since stopped paying any rent.

Garbage Heap

Says Shivram Gaekwad, "How can the owner come round to collect any rent when our huts are in such a sorry state? Last week a whole chunk of concrete collapsed in one of the toilets almost killing the man who had gone in!"

At Shyam Jalan Wadi, we come upon a huge heap of garbage which the 'rehvasis' claim is rarely touched by the municipality, even though it is within reach from both sides of the lane. No wonder so many of the slum-dwellers suffer from various illnesses. The only open plot of land here, which was to be converted into a garden for the use of the slum dwellers is being utilised by garage and used-cars dealer. This, the residents claim, is against municipality laws.

Our last visit is to Upendra Nagar, near Dadar Station. The entire colony nestles in a shallow trough next to the railway lines. More than 500 shanties line the sides of the trough, leaving the deepest portion bare. Water from the railway tracks flows into this pit which has degenerated into filthy black quagmire.

It is in such surroundings that even foodstuffs are prepared. In the narrow bylanes, full of slush and uncleared garbage, we come across a man preparing dosa dough. This is the stuff that will be later sold in the open market and consumed by the Bombayman. Carts of such food vendors line one end of the central pit.

'Mini Hell'

Because the shanties are built on a slightly lower level than the rest of the area, every monsoon becomes a mini hell for the slum-dwellers. Bemoans Ganpat Narain Chavan, "Hardly have the monsoons begun and our houses are flooded with water. At the height of the season, we have to wade through waist deep water." His sister Tarabai says, "Along with the water come creatures like snails, earthworms, and even toads. They even creep into the food we eat".

Last year, the Corporation had attempted to fill up the central pit by means of truck-loads of gravel and stones. This had checked the problem to some extent. But this year nothing has been done because of lack of funds.

As in the other slums in this Ward, garbage is not cleared daily from Upendra Nagar. Says B.P. Surve who has been a resident of the colony for the past twenty years. "It is only when we go to the municipality and lodge a complaint about the uncleared garbage that it is cleared. But who can afford to leave their daily tasks every second morning to go and plead for the clearance of the rubbish?"

VII

MACHIMARS: VICTIMS OF 'FISHY' DEAL

The approach to Machi Mar Nagar, the venue for our Ward by Ward Crusade, is marred by the smell of drying fish, assailing our nostrils, causing us to take an involuntary step backwards. This section of Mahim has been inhabited by fisherfolk for more than a century.

The huts lined the Mahim Creek on both sides of the highway between Mahim Church and Bandra. Perhaps it was because of the fact that these huts were placed in the vicinity of the airport that they came to be classified as eyesores by the rest of the city, and plans for their displacement began to be discussed.

It was not an easy task to demolish these huts. All attempts were vigorously repulsed by the hardy fisherfolk. Their consent for the demolishment proceedings was only obtained when the Government promised to provide quarters for all of them on the same spot, with a nominal rent of Rs. 25 per tenement.

Ramchandra Vinde, President of the Machi Mar Sangh who is addressed as Guruji by the other residents, explains how these simple folk were betrayed by the Government. The first blow fell when, instead of the promised Rs. 25, the rent was fixed at Rs. 42 for those in the below Rs. 250 income group, and Rs. 95 for those in the higher income group. As most of the residents earn less than Rs. 350 p.m., these charges appear exorbitant. The huts were demolished for the benefit of these backward classes, yet they now pay Rs. 78 as standard rent and Rs. 150 as economic.

These quarters, which fall under Municipal Ward No. 72, were constructed in two phases by the Housing Board, now known as BHADB. 14 buildings with 560 tenements were constructed in the first phase by the end of 1969, and nine double buildings comprising of 720 tenements were constructed in 1973.

The residents are unanimous that shoddy and adulterated materials were utilised during construction. Within a short span of 10 years, the buildings are literally coming apart. The J.G. Bodhe Samiti, appointed by the Maharashtra Government to scrutinise the work carried out by the BHADB has mentioned in its report that the construction of the Machimar Colony is one of the worst specimens.

The smell of faeces and urine mingles with that of the drying fish and pervades the entire colony. Leaking sewage pipes have been plaguing the residents from the beginning. Dirty stagnant pools provide excellent breeding ground for mosquitoes and flies.

"We are forced to keep the rear windows closed the whole year round," complains Dattaram Adalkar, a resident of building No. 17. Some of the residents are forced to cook their daily meals in a room where sewage water seeps in continuously. No scavenger has ever stepped in to clean the drains, as they are so chockful of dirt and filth, it would be impossible to force a way in.

A 24-hour water supply provides little solace to the residents. All the water tanks have deteriorated to little more than seives. The natural process of rusting has played havoc with the inferior quality iron of the tanks. Thus even with plentiful water supply, the residents are forced to get their water by drawing it from the tanks by bucket before it can seep out.

The peeling of plaster has become a normal phenomena by now. The ceilings constantly shed plaster. Last year, the ceiling of a flat in building No. 12 collapsed bringing down the fan and instantaneously killing a five-year-old girl who was sleeping

beneath it. Such tragedies are becoming more frequent with the
passage of time.

The Board takes note of all the complaints but does precious
little about them. A ground floor balcony was demolished last
September because it was said to be dangerous. The BHADB's
laxity is exemplified by their tardiness in carrying out repairs.
Till today the balcony remains unrepaired, a hazard to the infants of that floor.

As the buildings have been constructed on land which was
marshy once, the flooring displays a tendency to subside from
time to time. Jayaram Pandurang Marde, woefully displays the
gaping holes in his tenement. "Some of these pits, they cannot
even be called holes, are more than a foot in depth," he says,
"we do our best to repair them, by filling them with mud, topped
by gravel."

As with the flooring, so it is with the ceiling and terrace. The
terraces have been so badly tarred that every monsoon the residents of the top floor have no option but to fix tarpaulin or
plastic sheets across their ceilings. The bathrooms leak the most,
and residents are forced to take shelter under umbellas while
performing their daily ablutions.

Vinde Guruji bemoans the fact that there is no Municipal
school near the colony for its 3000 children. "The kids have to
traverse a distance of more than a mile to school at present,"
says Vinde. "We also feel the lack of a municipal clinic. Even
though there are two private dispensaries, the stiff charges are
beyond our means. We cannot afford such expensive medicines
even at the best of times." The closest municipal clinic is at
Mahim Bazar, a distance of more than two kilometres.

The colony seems to have been totally neglected by the various
authorities. For a colony of 7,000 residents, not even a single
public telephone has been provided, causing a great deal of in-
convenience. The BEST is also deaf to the appeals of the Machimar Nagar residents, who have been pressing for a bus-stop close
to the colony. At present, the residents have to choose between
the Bandra station bus-stop or the Mahim Church bus-stop.

These illiterate fisherfolk fall easy prey to the brokers who seek
to profit from the sea-food export trade. The fisherwomen spend
their own money on purchasing and cleaning the fish and deliver
it to the middlemen. They in turn sell the products to the cus-

tomers, and pocketing most of the money, they dole out a fraction of the sum to those to whom it is rightfully due.

Since all business is carried out orally, the exploited fisherwomen have to remain silent. In a recent case, N.C. Kapadia, a dealer in fish exports obtained Rs. 16,000/- worth of fish from some of the residents and has not returned a single paisa to date, alleges Vinde.

Of the original Khacharpatti Nagar, 25 families still remain in the huts which have served these fisherfolk for the past one hundred years. These huts have not changed with the times. One finds red tiles instead of the modern tin or asbestos roofing and cool green plantain saplings cluster around the entrance to this section of Khacharpatti Nagar. Unfortunately, the same problems of an overcrowded city plague the residents. Pointing to the row of dabbas beneath dry taps, Manorama Rangankar laments: "We have to be satisfied with whatever we get. These two taps serve more than 500 families that live here."

But it was the plight of the residents of Mahim Slope which we found to be the most pitiable. For years they have been living cheek-by-jowl with the sea, the only protection in their battle for survival being the wooden and stone barricades that they themselves have put up.

At high tide, the sea gently licks the wooden barricades, but with the onset of the monsoons the fury of the sea knows no bounds. Waves even bigger than the shanties crash down on the huts and with every virulent backwash, a couple of them break loose from their moorings and are destroyed.

Last year, more than 30 huts were washed away. Touched by their plight, Smt. Ahilyabai Rangnekar succeeded in getting the BHADB to sanction a sum of Rs. 7.5 lakhs for their rehabilitation in pucca housing. A year has elapsed with no signs of any activity for new houses for the Mahim Slope residents. Will the BHADB come to its senses only after a repetition of last year's tragedy?

PROFILES

I

I'VE NO FUTURE HERE

Ahmed Kassim Mukadam (43) is an odd-job man, which in reality means that he is out of a job most of the time. He repairs everything, from huts to sewing machines, in order to feed his family of seven children. He does not seem to have been too successful in this.

With what appears to be liquor staining his breath, Mukadam, berates his existence, an edge of desperation to his voice. At present residing in plot No. 10 at Malvani for the past four years, he previously used to live at Bandra near the old abattoir.

Is your mode of earning steady and well paying ?

Business is very difficult now. No one trusts you with any of their goods. They ask you to pay a deposit before for repairs. When I was at Bandra, things were much better and it used to be easy to scrape a living.

Knowing where you reside, do your customers still need to ask for a deposit ?

The hut in which I am presently staying is not mine. It belongs to friends who have gone to their native place and they have let me use it. I have been trying to get a small plot of land measuring 50-60 sq. meters but am not succeeding. I had lost my ration card and the authorities now allege that I got my duplicate through foul means.

What do most of the menfolk do for their monthly income?

Some of them have their own small businesses. Others work in private and Government offices or in factories and mills. Our women toil in the houses of the rich as 'ayahs'.

Coming to the actual living conditions of your slums, what are the timings of the water supply?

The water is available from six to eight in the mornings and between ten to one in the afternoons.

Is the water supplied clean and considerably germ free?

'Nahin saheb. Aram se kiden dekh sakte hain'. (You can see the worms with the naked eye.) We have to strain the water through a cloth before using it.

Are there enough taps amongst you?

No air. There are very few of them. The pressure is very low and in some taps there is no water at all. The toilets are also less in number. There is no water in the overhead tanks.

Is your present transport link with Malad railway station sufficient?

Yes, the bus service is good and regular. The frequency at peak hours is very high. The first bus starts at 4.30 in the morning from here. The last bus from Malad railway station is at 1.22 a.m.

What about the police? Is there a considerable amount of crime?

The situation is improving as there is a police station in our colony. But where do the poor get justice? 'Jiske pass paisa hain, uski hi sunai deti hain' (Only the one who has money is heard).

You have a large number of children, what about their education?

The last said about it the better. My eldest daughter, who is thirteen, cannot write her father's name yet. They are all promoted anyway.

In your line of infrequent jobs what future is there for you?

'Kuch nahin'. Though I was born and have lived all my life

in the city, sometimes I feel like leaving it and going back to my native place, Ratnagiri, and tilling land out there.

II

THE ORDEAL OF RUKMANI AND KESHAV

Rukmani (40) and Kheshav (45), both looking older than their age like most of the poor and downtrodden do, were ruthlessly cheated by fate for the second time when the Government's goons uprooted them from their home at Cuffe Parade's Jawaharnagar slum.

Keshav had a little plot of land in Hyderabad, which he sold to get the money to travel to the Gulf because someone promised to help him to go to Dubai for a job. He gave away whatever he collected from the sale of his plot, but when he reached Bombay to make the promised journey, he found the man had disappeared.

Forlorn and bereft of all they possessed, the couple and their two sons picked up courage and started life afresh in the 'zopadpatti' at Cuffe Parade more than two years ago. Their younger son, Bhaskar (8), was taken care of by Daulat Doongaji, Principal of the New Activity High School, under the National Sponsorship Programme, she gave him free education looked after all his needs. Another son was sent to Hyderabad by the National Sponsorship Committee to study in a boarding school.

The couple found work at the construction sites around Cuffe Parade. It looked like life began to flow smoothly once again when suddenly on Saturday, May 5, they were uprooted, their bag and baggage bundled off in a truck and taken to nowhere.

Bhaskar, who was schooling at Peddar Road, has now to give up the New Activity School because there is no way he can bus it from the god-forsaken area in Malad, where they have been dumped, all the way to Pedder Road.

The parents, of course, face the nightmare of jungle life without employment, with the rest of the victims of the city's slum dem olition project.

III

'I HATE MY WORK'

Harkumar (49) is a shoeshine at Veer Nariman Road, one of the countless whose only source of livelihood is a brush and boot polish. Overcoming his initial suspicion and reluctance, he pours his woes and problems on the city's pavement.

How long have you been in this profession ?

It has been for 25 long years that I am polishing shoes on the footpath. But it is 30 years that I have been in this city. I was born in Kerala and brought up in Coimbatore, which I left at the age of 19 to make my living here.

What did you do before you took up this job ?

I worked at the Tata Mills (Parel) as a canteen boy for five years, where I used to get a salary of Rs. 270 per month. It was a very good job, but as it was on temporary basis I had to quit. Since then I have taken to shoe shining.

How much does your monthly earnings amount to ?

If business is good I make Rs. 15 per day. On normal days I get about Rs. ten or seven after paying for the 'samaan'. I have Rs. three or four left with me.

Besides shoe shining I also do odd jobs for one Dr. Andya, like running errands for him, paying his bills, etc. For this he pays me Rs. 150 a month.

Do your earnings sufficiently meet your expenses ?

Not really. I have a wife and four children to look after. I stay in a 'kachha zopadi' at Sion. My neighbours and I are shelling out money to make our abode a 'pucca' one, prices are so high now that I have to think before I spend each paise.

During which part of the year does your business really pick up?

The winter is the best season. It is this time of the year that I earn the most. Since there is no business in the rainy season, I have to live on debts. And it is during the cold months that I can afford to pay back my debts.

In the locality where you reside, what are the problems you have to face ?

There is no hospital facilities in our area. The Municipal Hospital at Sion, which is close to my house, does not care for us. We are treated very badly, there is always a scarcity of medicines and most often we are given wrong treatment.

I lost one of my daughters because of their neglect. Since then, I have never stepped there I now go to the G.T. Hospital, a much better place.

Do you have to pay any 'hafta' to goondas for carrying on business ?

No such problems. We are about 25 shoeshine boys on the Veer Nariman Road and we keep good relations with each other. We are permanently placed here and allow no other 'boot polishwala' in this area, nor are we permitted anywhere else.

What about your children'? Do you intend to educate them or do you want your son in your profession ?

The truth is that I myself am not very happy about this job of mine, then why should I drag my son into it. I wish to work as a peon in some office and leave boot polishing.

I will educate my children, specially my son. I had admitted two of my children in the Municipal School in Sion, but after some days they were thrown out, with the excuse that they had never been admitted. So now I have made arrangements in the Tamil Municipal School in Matunga.

If your hopes are not realised will you go back to your home town?

'Ji nahin! Why should I? I have no one of my own except some of my wife's relatives. My parents died long back. Besides the conditions are no better there. The 'zopadas' in Tamil Nadu are also very expensive—Rs. 40/- a month. I go only for a short holiday and that too for my wife's sake.

JANATA COLONY : AN EXAMPLE OF EVICTION

In the State of Maharashtra in November 1975, an ordinance, No. XVIII 1975 was promulgated. In the following year it became the 'Maharashtra Vacant Land Act, 1976'. By this act all government and municipal lands inhabited by slums were declared vacant and all structures on them deemed unauthorised. This act conferred extreme powers on the government officials to take steps to evict the people living on these lands. The officials were not obliged to give any notice to the residents regarding evictions. Furthermore, any resistance to the eviction by the residents was and is deemed to be a punishable offence. We have talked about it in some detail in the preceding chapters. What follows here is an account of the eviction of Janata Colony— one of the three biggest slums in Bombay, in May 1976. The eviction took place duing the Emergency. The residents had filed a petition to the Shah Commission enquiring into the emergency excesses. The petition speaks for itself. We are giving below a gist of the sordid drama enacted in our city some years ago.

"In 1949 (or 1950) the Bombay Municipal Corporation decided to transfer different 'jhopadpattis' (slums) of Bombay to Mankhurd. In accordance with the decision the Bombay Municipal Corporation acquired land at Mankhurd. In 1950-51 (when Mr. Morarji Desai was the Chief Minister) different slums of Bombay were demolished and shifted to Mankhurd in the basin of a hillock on the Sion-Trombay Road. The uprooted persons were assured that it would be their permanent place of residence. They made this inhabitable land habitable. They were allotted 300 sq. ft. each to build their houses. The place was named Janata Colony. In the beginning the inhabitants were put to great hardship. They used to fetch the drinking water from far-off places. However, they started their new life with the satisfaction that they would not be uprooted again.

"Over a period of 25 years the Janata Colony developed into a kind of a township by itself. An inventory of some of the structures and activities of the then Janata Colony would present the following picture:

Hutments	7,450
Electricity, private connections for lighting	1,500
Electricity, connections for commercial purposes	150
Mosques	5
Temples	6
Churches	2
Schools	4
Police Station	1
Municipal Office	1
Dispensaries	17
Eating Places .. .. .. over	20
Municipal Markets	2
Ration Shops	4
Private Municipal Water Connections ..	21
Public Municipal Water Taps ..	44
Drinking Water Wells	5
Public Latrines	220 seats

"Many of the residents worked in the city, but there was a considerable volume of activity within and nearby places of the colony itself. Some details of occupations are as follows :

Men working in BARC complex ..	1,200
Dock workers .. .. .. over	2,000
B.M.C. workers .. .. .. over	600
State Government workers	80
Central Government workers	45
Mill workers .. .. .. over	170
Major shops, including barbers, tailors, eating places, grocers etc. ..	120

Small shops (usually in the same hut in which the owner resided)	..	400
Power looms		2
Furniture shops		15
Flour mills		10
Jari works (Embroidery)		260
Ready-made Garment works ..		10
Small scale industries .. .. over		65
Women working in the BARC buildings as domestic servants		360

"As shown above the people inhabiting Janata Colony started cottage industries, built churches, temples and mosques. It was a real township in that sense. In spite of people belonging to different faiths living at one place, not a single case of communal disharmony was witnessed in the 25 years of the history of the colony. All the 70,000 inhabitants of the colony who professed different faiths lived in peace and harmony. It really had a cosmopolitan character.

"In 1952 the Bhabha Atomic Research Centre (B.A.R.C.) was established on the other side of the hillock near the Janata Colony. In 1952 itself, the workers who were working for the BARC settled near the Janata Colony on a site called 'Chikolari'. During the same year the Government wanted to give away the Janata Colony land to some oil company but the Municipal Corporation did not approve of it. On 15th January 1963 for the first time the Bombay Municipal Corporation took up the matter of shifting the Janata Colony. Dr. Bhabha, the BARC chief had assured the delegation of the Janata Colony that if ever the colony was shifted to some other place the BARC would provide pucca houses to the affected persons. Afterwards, Dr. Vikram Sarabhai and other important persons also issued press statement to the effect that the Janata Colony people would be provided pucca houses worth 44 crores.

"In 1965-66 a survey of Janata Colony was conducted by the BARC. And in 1966 BARC advised the Janata Colony people to form Co-operative Societies. In 1966 construction of quarters for the BARC staff began near the Janata Colony. In 1969-70 the Janata Colony people submitted a plan of 4,500 houses to the then Minister of Urban Development of the Government of Maharashtra Mr. P. G. Kher. In 1971 the then Chief Minister Shri V. P. Naik declared that all the person residing at Janata Colony will be given propriety rights of the houses in the Janata Colony. The Chief Minister also asked the residents of the Janata Colony to deposit Rs. 1,600/- each within three months. In this area there was a Congress dominated association called "Mankhurd Janata Colony Residents' Association". This Association formed a co-operative housing society under the guidance and leadership of Raja Kulkarni, M.P., V. K. Tembe, M.L.A., H. R. Shishodre, Municipal Councillor and the President of the Dock Workers Union S. R. Kulkarni. Through the connivance and deceit of the leadership in this society such persons were also included who were not the residents of the Janata Colony. Rs. 80,000/- were collected from the members of the society and deposited with the BARC. In 1973-74 BMC declared that all the unauthorised structures of the Janata Colony would be legalised but this declaration did not materialise. On 10th December, 1974 a notice was posted in the Municipal Office of the colony for the shifting of the Janata Colony to Cheeta Camp and thus clearing the area.

"A deputation of the colony met the Chief Minister of Maharashtra at Nagpur and submitted a memorandum to him regarding the shifting of the colony. On 1st February 1975, Maharashtra's Minister for Housing, Prabhakar Kunte advised the BMC not to shift the Janata Colony. Congress leaders once again formed a Co-operative Housing Society. This society again included such persons who were not the residents of the Janata Colony. The chief of the BARC declared in a press statement that the site of the Janata Colony would be utilised for constructing a swimming pool, theatre and other recreation centres. In April, 1975 during the Chief Ministership of S. B. Chavan rumours went around about the shifting of the Janata Colony. On 11 April a morcha was taken to the Council Hall against the move. This was a 30,000 strong morcha of the Janata Colony residents. The Chief Minister S. B. Chavan told the leaders of the morcha that the Central Government thought that, the Janata Colony was a danger to the National Security and that the State Government was under constant pressure to shift it. But he promised to delay the shifting for some more days. Dr. Sethna said in a press Statement that if proper arrangements were not made for the accommodation of our scientists they would seek employment abroad. His implied reference was towards the Janata Colony.

"On 20th May 1975 thousands of SRP Jawans surrounded the Janata Colony. The State Government and the BMC were passive observers. The children and women-folk of the Janata Colony blocked their way by squatting on the road. On 23rd May 1975 the High Court by an Order stayed the shifting of the colony. On 16th June, the High Court ordered the BMC to issue individual notices instead of collective notices. On 5th August the BMC issued notices to the residents but most persons did not receive the notices. On 29th December 1975 an enquiry conducted by the BMC was completed. The enquiry officers did not register that the residents were willing to vacate the area provided they were given alternative accommodation. The Officers simply wrote down that the residents were ready to shift. On 2nd February 1976 a suit was filed in the City Civil Court and a Stay Order was obtained. 23rd August 1976 was fixed for the hearing. On 25th February 1976 the BMC appealed against the case of 2nd February and the Court dismissed the case. On 25th February itself the High Court gave a Stay Order against the Vacant Land Order. On 26th February 1976 BMC got the stay order of 25th declared null and void but the original suit was not affected. On 15th March 1976 a petition was filed in the High Court against the Vacant Land Order of 13.2.1976 and the judgement of 25.2.1976. After some days, only 3 days' Stay Order was granted. On 23rd March 1976 an appeal was filed in the Supreme Court. It granted stay till 5th April 1976. On 5th April the Supreme Court ordered that the Janata Colony people should be provided with more facilities and then shifted from the place after a month. The State Government and the BMC were contacted in the light of the Supreme Court judgement but neither the Government nor the BMC paid any attention to it. They were stuck to their original programme. On 13th May 1976 the SRP and Civil Police surrounded the Janata Colony. On 14th May 1976 an Appeal was filed in the High Court because the Government and the BMC did not pay any attention to the Order of the Supreme Court but the High Court neither dismissed the Appeal nor allowed it. It merely kept it in abeyance. On 16th May 1976 a deputation of the colony requested the BPCC President Mr. Rajani Patel, and BMC Commissioner Mr. B. G. Deshmukh to postpone the shifting till the end of the monsoon. Mr. Rajani Patel refused to do anything whereas Mr. Deshmukh wanted Rs. 15,000/- to be paid by the slum dwellers towards the expenditure incurred on the police arrangements. He was to give only one week's time, that too after the payment of Rs. 15,000/-. The poor residents could not afford such a big amount for only a week's lease of life.

"And finally it was on the 17th of May 1976 that the forcible shifting operation of the Janata Colony began. It was not an easy operation for the Government and the police. There were severe lathi charges by the police on the residents of the colony. Houses were just destroyed and demolished ruthlessly. The forcible shifting of the people from Janata Colony to the new place at Cheeta Camp began in the trucks provided by the BMC. The whole operation took nearly 25 days and was completed by the 10th of June 1976. Every family was allotted a site on the basis of leave and licence whereas at Janata Colony there was no leave and licence system. In Cheeta Camp the rent was fixed at Rs. 20/- whereas at Janata Colony it was Rs. 3.25.

"On 17th May 1976 itself the people who shifted to the Cheeta Camp held a big rally at the site of the Janata Colony and protested against the inhuman treatment meted out to them by the BMC Officials. Some persons were arrested and cases were filed against them. On the 1st June 1976 while the eviction and demolition operation was going on there were heavy rains which continued for some days sweeping away all the belongings and building materials of the poor residents. At both places, in Janata Colony as well as in Cheeta Camp, women and children experienced terrible hardships as there was no roof over their heads. In Janata Colony, their houses were demolished and at Cheeta Camp, their houses were not as yet complete. The BMC authorities did not provide enough house sites in the Cheeta Camp. A man named Abdul Hameed committed suicide out of sheer frustration.

"According to the Bombay Municipal Corporation, shifting of the Janata Colony was necessary because the BARC needed the land. The Chairman of BARC, Dr. Sethna, on different occasions, had expressed the same view. As stated earlier he said that a swimming pool, a theatre and recreation places would be provided on the land for those who lived in the BARC colony. He advanced the theory of accommodation for the scientists attached to BARC failing which there would be a brain-drain from this country. For the benefit and recreation of a privileged few, 70,000 persons were uprooted.

"Though the removal of Janata Colony was planned much earlier, the authorities found the most appropriate and opportune time of implementing their plan during the days of the Emergency when nobody could air their grievances nor could they seek the protection of the law. The Janata Colony people had to undergo the cumulative loss of about Rs. 10 crores while they were compensated by a paltry amount of Rs. 400/- each."

The eviction of the Janata Colony was neither exceptional nor an emergency excess alone. It has been a regular periodic feature. As such there is no guarantee that they will not be evicted from their present dwelling in Cheeta Camp after few years. It is a clever way of developing an unproductive land and of appreciating (increasing) their value at no cost.

Cheeta Camp—the new relocated slum settlement, is situated at a distance of nearly five kilometers away from the original Janata Colony site (present BARC compound) on Sion-Trombay road. It is a low lying marshy backwaters area. In 1976 when the Janata Colony was being relocated on this new site the whole area appeared unworthy of human settlement. Total lack of planning marked the beginning of this unfortunate relocation process. The details of the area, settlement plots, density etc. as specified in the official records at the time of relocation were as below :

1. Total plot area   :   6,52,250 sq. ft.   14.97 acres)
2. Total number of plots :   4593
   (a) Residential   :   4199
   (b) Industrial   :   327
   (c) Social   Service
        Institutions   :   13
   (d) Non-classified   :   54
3. Total population   :   21, 804
4. Total plot area under   5,95,350 sq. ft.
   residential use   :   i.e., 13.67 acres.

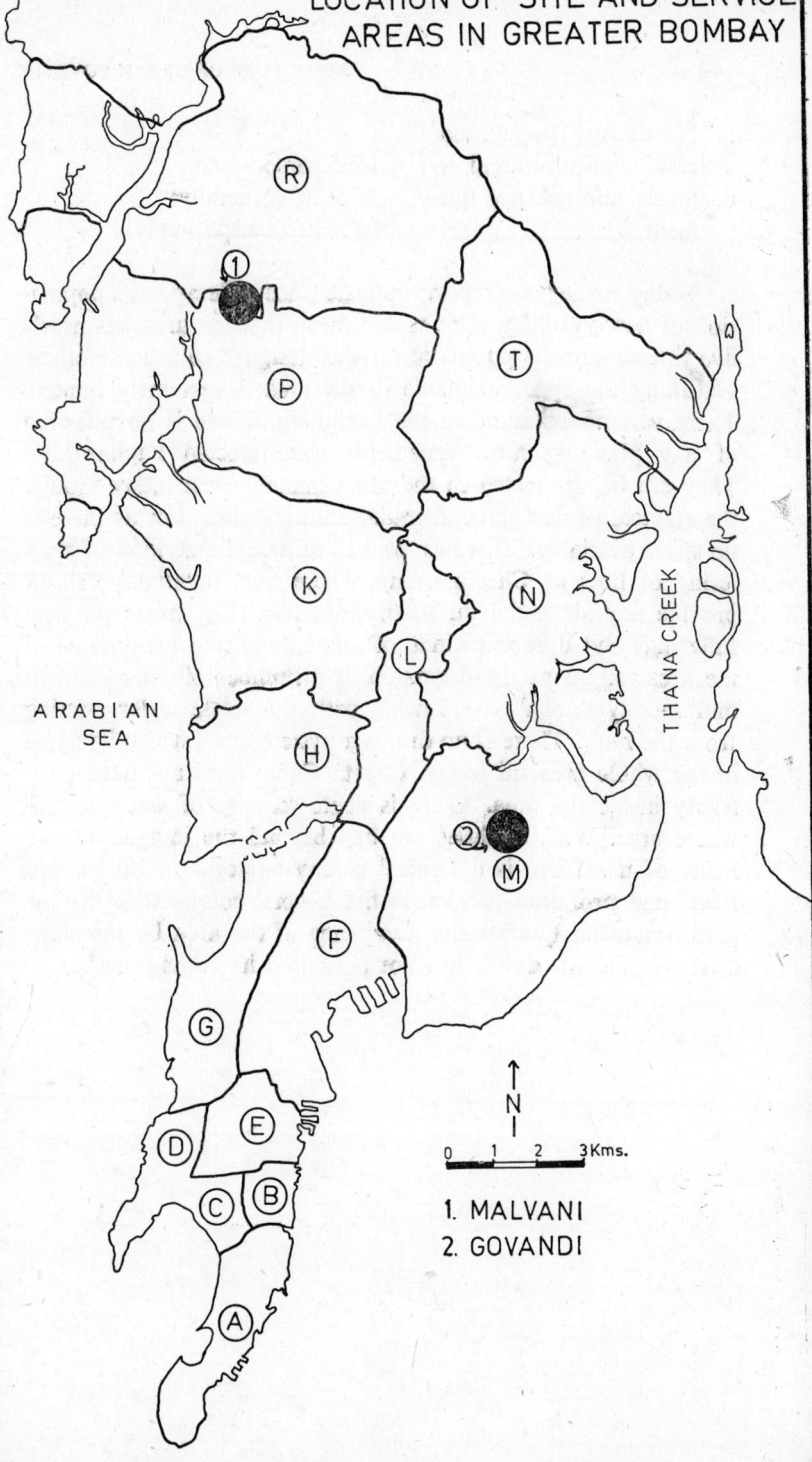

LOCATION OF 'SITE AND SERVICE
AREAS IN GREATER BOMBAY

R

1

T

P

ARABIAN
SEA

K

N

L

H

THANA CREEK

2.
M

F

G

N

0 1 2 3 Kms.

E

D

1. MALVANI
2. GOVANDI

C B

A

5. Net density (population/
   residential plot area)   :   1595 persons/acre
6. Space allotted per hut-   15' × 10' (generally)
   ment   . :   10' × 10' (exceptionally)

Today as the press reports indicate Cheeta Camp has a population of nearly a lakh. This would mean that the area has nearly
five times more the population it was designed to accommodate.
Naturally the space available in the area is extremely limited.
There was no planning in the beginning. There is no question
of any planning now. Tenements were erected haphazardly.
They are being erected in the same manner even today though
the chances of new huts emerging are much less now as there is
no space available. This has resulted in an extreme kind of clus-
tering of huts at Cheeta Camp. These huts invariably fail to
provide any air and light to the inmates. This causes physical
sufferings and different kinds of ailments to the inhabitants of
the area. Right at the door-step of a number of huts one can
find muddy "nalla" overflowing with the waste water coming
from the huts. There is no drainage system at all worth its name
in the whole area till today. Cheeta Camp does not have electricity inside the area. There is acute scarcity of water in the
whole area. W.C. facilities are bad beyond the imagination of
many of us. There is a Lepers' colony adjacent to this camp.
BMC had promised to remove the Lepers' colony to a distant
place immediately after the occupancy of the area by the slum
dwellers. To this day it has not honoured its commitments.

CONCLUDING OBSERVATIONS

This study indicates that there is an organic link between urban policy and emergence, growth and proliferation of slums in a city. The study also indicates that the phenomenon of slum cannot be conceived simply as an overflow of rural poverty. Nor can one explain it in terms of culture of poverty'. As our evaluation of the programmes relating to the relocation and improvement of slums in Bombay has shown the slum question cannot be discussed in isolation. The whole range of questions pertaining to the slum settlements in a city is inextricably linked with the housing question. The question of housing in turn can be discussed meaningfully only when we take into consideration the land available in a city for this purpose. Land exists as private property and it comes to be the most precious commodity. It is equally precious as extremely essential consumer goods in short supply. The rich, the middle classes and the poor all need land for use and redevelopment. The rich are always in advantageous position. Either they own land or they have resources to buy it. They can use it as they consider it profitable. Up to a point some sections of the middle-classes can also manage to have access to land and required space for housing. As their members go down the economic hierarchy they find it increasingly difficult to accommodate themselves physically in a city. For the poor any legal occupancy of land is out of question. They do not have the capacity to buy land and required space for their housing. And the city though needs them as hands, as labour for its industrial and commercial enterprises and for hundreds of kinds of services required for its maintenance as a civic place, does not take the responsibility of accommodating them. Left with no option, the poor in a city squat on such vacant lands where, to begin with, there is no resistance or there is such resistance as they can manage. This is how slums and squatter-settlements emerge.

A city tolerates its slum dwellers up to the period they can be utilized as cheap labour and the maintenance of their habitat does not involve any significant expenditure of public funds. This situation does not last long. Over a period of time the slums and squatter-settlements grow and proliferate and the city now finds this reserve army of cheap labour well beyond its utilizing capacity. This development has repercussions elsewhere on the city system. The 'marginal' settlements become the home of a vast majority of the city's population and pose a threat to its property system—the lands on which these settlements are located are considered as 'invaded areas'. The mechanisms for the social control of the slum dwellers threaten to fail now. Increasingly insanitary slums are considered as breeding grounds of diseases, various types of crimes and unstructured violence. Now the unemployed squatters and slum dwellers get transformed into dangerous parasites. The city cannot tolerate its slum dwellers any more. It would like to dispense with them. But it cannot. Their labour is still required to run the industrial and commercial enterprises, their services are still needed to maintain the civic system. It cannot separate the employed slum dwellers from those unemployed and thus keep one section in and throw the other section out. Slums come to stay in the city—howsoever degraded their physical existence be.

The city, as if suddenly awakened to this critical situation, calls it a crisis—the 'slum crisis' and starts seeking 'solutions' for its resolutions. Programmes like relocation, up-gradation and improvement of slums and squatter-settlements are designed as 'solutions' to 'urban problems' and 'slum crisis', as help extended to the 'economically weaker section' of the urban population. These programmes are designed within the matrix of the private property system that operates in the city. For example no land tenure is granted to the slum dwellers. They are treated simply as passive recipients of such social programmes and economic aid. As experience has shown such programmes as mentioned above seldom meet with success. Programmes relating to upgradation and improvement of slums are, in fact, never implemented seriously and honestly. Programme of relocation of slums eventually emerges as a programme of demolition and eviction of slums. This is a desperate move that a city takes and it entails untold misery for the affected slum dwellers.

To substantiate the above generalizations we give below the facts that emerge from our study of the relocation and improvement of slums in the metropolis of Bombay. We will enumerate these facts briefly and conclude our report.

1. The total population of Greater Bombay is now approximately over 8 million. The projected population for Greater Bombay in 2100 A.D. is around 15 million. Over half the present population (approximately 4.7 million) lives in slums. The projected population of slum dwellers in the city at the turn of this century, given the existing conditions, would be around 8 million, a number nearing the existing total population of Bombay. About a quarter of the total population of the city lives in dilapidated buildings. A large chunk of this population is going to be slum dwellers tomorrow. Less than one per cent of the people in the city live on the less used pavements, representing the most wretched section of the urban population.

2. Slums are the result of structural inequalities in society. They have grown over the years owing to the industrial and commercial expansion in the city. People have been migrating from nearby and far-off areas, rural areas functioning as the main depository of the supply of cheap labour to the city since its emergence as an industrial place, in search of jobs. The city is able to absorb them as cheap labour but is not built to accommodate them. Highly congested shanty structures known as *jhopadpatties* built illegally on vacant land in the city are the only mode of accommodation available to the migrant workers.

3. These slum dwellers make significant and massive contribution to the economic life of the city. Be it the formal sector or the so-called informal sector of the economy, they provide cheap labour to run them. They provide cheap labour for the service sector of the city. They work as sweepers and scavengers, as household servants and menials. Without them, the city's economy would grind to a halt. And the city would plunge into chaos if they stopped working.

4. Urban planning in general and housing programmes in

particular are always marked by an ideology which determines the course of urban development. Planning of Bombay has not only been lopsided and without a vision to foresee the future needs of this city, it has also been highly discriminatory to the poor in terms of making provisions for their accommodation facilities and the basic services needed for their everyday existence. So far planners of the city have been mainly concerned with the green and the prosperous belts of the city. They have never gone to the poorer section of the people. Planning for the poor is yet to emerge.

5. Population of the city has been growing at about four per cent per annum for the last two decades. The concomitant improvement required in its infrastructure particularly housing has not kept pace with the population growth. As against the estimated annual need of 60,000 housing units the supply of 'formal' housing units has been around 15,000 to 20,000 in the recent past. Over fifty per cent of its population living in slums, is a manifestation not only of this gap between the need and the supply in the 'formal' sector of housing but also of the total unconcern and lack of consideration for 'equity' in the provision of public housing. In terms of formulating even seemingly progressive policy towards meeting the housing needs of the poorer sections in the city, the performance of the State Government has been dismal. The result being that an enormous population lives in appalling conditions in the city's slums.

6. The State Government has increasingly tilted its policy towards the builders, speculators and owners of large tracts of land in the city. A look at the fate of the Urban Land (Ceiling and Regulation) Act of 1976 in the city makes it clear. The main provisions of this Act have been violated by the office of the State Government itself through various ways of circumvention and manipulation of the Act in favour of the land owners, builders, real estate speculators and the rich in the city. The Act has, thus, failed completely in achieving its primary objective—to make land available to genuinely poor sections. With the promulgation of the Act, the prices of land and flats have shot up enormously proving quite detrimental to the poorer section in the city. The nexus that exists between the rich in the city and the higher echelons of bureaucracy and the politicians belies any possibility of a people-oriented rational housing policy.

7. The Maharashtra Slum Areas (Improvement, Clearance and Redevelopment) Act, 1971 and The Maharashtra Slum Improvement Board Act, 1973 have not only failed in redeveloping the slum localities and improving the quality of life there, they have emerged, in effect, as a programme of eviction and demolition of slums. As the Municipal records show only a small section of the slum population in the city was covered under the improvement programme. Bulk of the slum population has remained without any civic amenities provided for in the 1971 and 1973 Acts. In slum colonies where amenities like latrines, water taps, drainage, street lights etc. are provided, there is hardly any attempt to keep these services in order. In a number of cases such facilities are in awfully bad condition and out of use. Neither the local people nor the Municipal Corporation seem to be concerned about the repair and maintenance of these amenities. Besides, the vast size of the slum population poses operational and financial difficulties. No monitoring and evaluation is done once the facilities are provided and thus when the population increases in an improved slum, proportionate increase in facilities does not take place. This results in over-burdening of the existing services.

8. The environmental improvement programme in the city is scuttled. The fear is that giving basic amenities would amount to an indirect recognition of 'illegal' occupants. Complicated procedures, indecision, delay, red-tapism etc., that occur on the surface in the context of improvement programmes are directly related to the question of land. Shortage of land in the city is a slogan raised by the private landlords, industrialists and the vested interests in the State Government. Figures relating to the vacant land in the city reveal that there is more than sufficient land to house the slum and pavement dwellers not only now but also up to a point in future.

9. Developments during the course of last ten years make it clear that the Government has shifted its policy from "alternative accommodation" (1971 Act) to "alternative site" (1973 Act) to enable it to evict and demolish large number of slums in the city. In the name of 'public interest', the Government has virtually transformed the slum improvement and redevelopment programme into a slum eviction and demolition programme. Since 1975 demolition and eviction of slums in the city has taken

place on an unprecedented scale almost invariably through the use of brutal force. The new sites for the resettlement of the evicted slums appear attractive on paper. But the actual physical conditions obtaining on such new sites are appalling. The result being that only a tiny section of the evicted slum dwellers have so far gone to these sites. A large number of them are squatting again either on the old sites or elsewhere in the city in a much more wretched condition.

10. The growing resistance of the slum dwellers and the protests organised by some political groups in opposition led to the introduction of "The Maharashtra Vacant Lands (Prohibition of Unauthorised Structures and Summary Eviction) Act, 1975". The purpose of this Act was to legitimize eviction and demolition of slums. Dissolving the Bombay Housing Board of 1948, the Bombay Building Repairs and Reconstruction Board of 1969 and the Maharashtra Slum Improvement Board of 1973, a new body called the Maharashtra Housing and Area Development Authority (MHADA) came into being in 1977. MHADA carries the responsibility of helping the Government to formulate developmental plans for cities in the State. Housing plans prepared for Bombay are based on the zoning laws which reminds one of the rigid zoning regulations and effective segregation of the rich and the poor practiced during the colonial period. These plans are not based on the actual requirements of the city's population. Improbable standards are set for amenities which cannot be met. This obviates the need for providing any amenities at all. For instance, the zoning laws stipulate a minimum plot size of 330 sq. meters, far larger than any house the poor can afford. Fifteen per cent of the plot must be open. The maximum permissible density is of 100 plots per net acre. Building plans must be designed by architects, and must be implemented by the contractors. All these regulations can only permit flats and bungalows which the poor and also a large section of the middle-classes cannot afford. This is on the one side. On the other side the slum upgradation programmes do not give any right to shelter. None of the Acts referred to earlier provides for any security of tenure to the slum dwellers. On the contrary the various legislations in force arm the Government to deal 'firmly' and 'effectively' with 'unauthorised development' in the city. The latest in the armoury of the Government is an Ordinance promulgated by

the Governor of Maharashtra in the month of June, 1983. This Ordinance amends the Maharashtra Regional and Town Planning Act, 1966 and provides for 'deterrent penalties' and gives 'speedy powers for demolition, discontinuance and removal' of 'unauthorised development'. The penalty for the so-called 'unauthorised development' has been increased from a fine to a three-year term of imprisonment. Thus building a hut on any vacant land in the city is a cognizable criminal offence. Any slum dweller under this charge can now be arrested 'without a warrant' and 'the offence is non-bailable'. Slum dwellers cannot obstruct demolitions in any way. Such acts are 'criminal' and will now carry a one-year term of imprisonment and a thousand rupees fine. Thus over fifty per cent of the population of this metropolis is entirely outside the protection of the law as regards their accommodation and exis ence.

We conclude our report reiterating our view that the slum problem is a part of the overall crisis generated by our present industrial and urban policy and unless there is a radical departure from this policy it has no real and effective solution. Schemes formulated for the welfare of the poor in the city by scholars of liberal persuasion and sympathetic administrators can perhaps work as temporary ameliorative measures if implemented sincerely and honestly. The tragedy is even that is not in sight.

APPENDIX

Tables on
A profile of 'relocated' and 'improved' slums

I

MIGRATION PATTERN

Distribution of household heads by reasons for coming to Bombay

Reasons/slum	Bharat Nagar	Hanu-man Tekdi	Golibar	Worli	Total
Seeking employment	73	93	35	45	246
Since birth in Bombay	11	12	12	14	49
Surplus members at home	33	6	22	1	62
Does not want to work as agricultural labourer	6	2	3	2	13
Transferred	0	1	0	0	1
Unhealthy relationships at native place	0	2	2	0	4
Debt, bondage at native place	17	2	6	0	25
Total	140	118	80	62	400

Distribution of families by State of Domicile

State/Slum	Bharat Nagar	Hanu- man Tekdi	Golibar	Worli	Total
Maharashtra	23	50	27	53	153
Gujarat	3	8	5	0	16
U.P.	27	18	42	4	91
M.P.	4	0	0	0	4
A.P.	5	22	0	4	31
Bihar	2	1	0	0	3
Karnataka	1	7	2	0	10
Tamil Nadu	10	2	0	0	12
Kerala	0	2	0	0	2
West Bengal	0	0	1	0	1
Orissa	0	0	1	0	1
Delhi	5	0	0	1	6
Punjab	60	3	0	0	63
Goa	0	3	1	0	4
Nepal	0	2	0	0	2
Pakistan	0	0	1	0	1
Total	140	118	80	62	400

Distribution of families by period of stay in various places

Place/Period	1—5 years	6—10 years	11—15 years	16—20 years	21—25 years	26—30 years	31—35 years	36+ years
Place of Birth	14	26	71	123	73	37	9	26
First place (after leaving birth place)	118	105	30	5	4	—	—	—
Second place	27	11	6	4	3	2	1	—
Third place	14	2	1	1	—	—	—	—
Fourth place	8	3	2	1	—	—	—	—
Fifth place	4	1	—	—	—	—	—	—

Note : 21 persons did not respond to this question.

Distribution of families by duration of stay in Bombay

Duration/Slum	Bharat Nagar	Hanu-man Tekdi	Golibar	Worli	Total
Since birth	14	15	12	14	55
1 year	—	5	—	—	5
1—3 years	1	1	—	—	2
3—5 years	6	4	3	—	13
5—10 years	15	18	3	5	41
10 years+	104	75	62	43	284
Total	140	118	80	62	400

Household heads and reasons for moving from place to place

Moves	Reasons								Total
	Due to Demolition	After Marriage	For Education	Due to Debt	Due to Troubles*	Temporary Accommodation at Previous Place	For Business	Due to Unemployment	
Nil	47	........BORN IN THE SLUM.........							47
Exactly one	77	16	6	6	10	8	35	104	262
Exactly two	15	3	3	0	12	1	14	6	54
Exactly three	4	1	1	0	2	1	7	2	18
Exactly four	6	0	1	0	5	0	2	0	14
Exactly five	2	0	1	0	0	0	1	1	5
Total	47 104	20	12	6	29	10	59	113	400

*Troubles include fights and unhealthy relationships.
Mean move per person=1.26, Mode is 1.09, Median is 1.08.

Heads of households by the reasons for their willingness to shift to native place

Reasons/Slum	Bharat Nagar	Hanu-man Tekdi	Golibar	Worli	Total
Family settled there	3	19	2	2	28
Want permanent job or a business	22	9	9	1	41
Due to sickness	0	2	0	0	2
Climatic and living conditions better at native place	14	19	15	24	72
Eviction	0	2	0	3	5
Have land and home at native place	3	6	3	2	11
Cost of living less in in native place	0	9	1	3	13

Number of persons (heads) willing = 175
Not willing = 188
No response = 37

Distribution of household heads by the reasons for their unwillingness to shift to native place

Reasons/Slum	Bharat Nagar	Hanu-man Tekdi	Golibar	Worli	Total
Family settled here	56	7	7	3	73
Employment prospects more in Bombay	7	19	7	7	40
Religious constraints	3	2	17	7	29
Financial problems	2	2	2	2	8
Political reasons	7	3	7	0	17
Accommodation problem	2	3	2	1	8
Job not available there	9	1	3	0	13

Number of persons (heads) willing to shift=175
Not willing to shift=188
No response= 37

Distribution of families by caste

Caste/Slum	Bharat Nagar	Hanu-man Tekdi	Golibar	Worli	Total
Scheduled Caste	74	21	12	25	132
Scheduled Tribe	0	10	3	4	17
O.B.C.	3	22	23	6	54
Others	63	65	42	27	197
Total	140	118	80	62	400

Distribution of families by religion

Religion/Slum	Bharat Nagar	Hanu-man Tekdi	Golibar	Worli	Total
Hindu	86	97	65	43	291
Christian	2	6	7	0	15
Muslim	52	14	8	5	79
Sikh	0	1	0	0	1
Neo-Buddhists	0	0	0	14	14
Jains;	0	0	0	0	0
Total	140	118	80	62	400

Distribution of families by mother tongue

Mother Tongue/ Slum	Bharat Nagar	Hanu-man Tekdi	Golibar	Worli	Total
Marathi/Konkani	5	49	27	49	130
Hindi	92	26	42	3	163
Urdu	30	4	6	5	45
Gujarati	4	7	3	0	14
Bengali	0	0	1	0	1
Oriya	0	0	1	0	1
Telugu	1	20	0	5	26
Kannada	0	6	0	0	6
Malayalam	0	2	0	0	2
Tamil	8	2	0	0	10
Nepali	0	2	0	0	2
Total	140	118	80	62	400

II SOCIAL CHARACTERISTICS

Distribution of family members by age, sex and marital status (all slums)

Age (years)	1—10		11—15		16—25		26—35		36—45		46—55		56—65		66—75		75+		Total		Grand Total
Marital Status	M	S	M	S	M	S	M	S	M	S	M	S	M	S	M	S	M	S	M	S	
Male adults	—	—	—	—	63	122	159	24	135	1	63	0	21	1	7	0	1	0	449	148	597
Female adults	—	—	—	—	120	60	147	1	68	0	29	0	14	3	3	0	0	0	381	64	445
Male children	—	239	—	108	—	—	—	—	—	—	—	—	—	—	—	—	—	—	—	347	347
Female children	—	246	2	93	—	—	—	—	—	—	—	—	—	—	—	—	—	—	2	339	341
Male guests	—	1	—	—	—	1	1	—	1	—	—	—	—	—	—	—	—	—	2	2	4
Female guests	—	2	—	—	—	1	1	—	1	—	—	—	—	—	—	—	—	—	2	3	5
Total	—	488	2	201	183	184	308	25	205	1	92	0	35	4	10	0	1	0	836	903	1739

M=Married   S=Single (never married)

III

OCCUPATIONAL STRUCTURE

Parental occupation of the respondents

Occupation/Slum	Bharat Nagar	Hanu-man Tekdi	Golibar	Worli	Total
Primary	30	70	40	29	169
Landless Labourer	3	2	1	9	15
Manufacturing	4	9	6	6	25
Water Supply, Electricity etc.	0	1	1	0	2
Service Industry	8	10	3	1	22
Trade and Commerce	14	6	15	2	37
Transportation	0	2	0	1	3
Construction Works	0	5	3	0	8
Personal Services	8	1	3	6	18
Manual Labourer	63	2	2	4	71
Domestic Servant	2	3	3	0	8
No Response/ Not Specified	8	7	3	4	22
Total	140	118	80	62	400

Test of independence of income and occupational status

Income (in Rs.) (mid-points)	Unskilled Worker		Self-Employed		Skilled Workers		Total
50	33	(23)	4	(5)	4	(13)	41
150	62	(54)	12	(11)	21	(30)	95
250	54	(57)	10	(11.5)	36	(32)	100
350	67	(67)	13	(13.7)	39	(38)	119
450	29	(36)	6	(7)	29	(20)	64
550	7	(10)	3	(2)	8	(6)	18
650	4	(5)	1	(1)	3	(3)	8
750	3	(3)	2	(1)	1	(2)	6
850	1	(2)	0	(.3)	2	(.7)	3
950	0	(2)	1	(.3)	2	(.7)	3
1050	0	(1)	1	(.2)	1	(.6)	2
Total	260		53		146		459

Figures in brackets are the expected or theoretical frequencies $x^2=37.45$. At 20 degrees of freem x^2 at 0.05 level of significance is 31.410. Hence $x^2_{0.05} < x^2$ (calculated value) i.e., we reject the hypothesis that Income and Occupational status are independent, i.e., we conclude that the three sections of workers do not enjoy the same income level. Skilled workers and the self-employed get more income by virtue of their occupational potential and status.

Distribution of families by the annual rent being paid by them

Rent/Slum	Bharat Nagar	Hanu-man Tekdi	Golibar	Worli	Total
Re. 1—100	—	3	6	—	9
Rs. 101—200	16	4	26	4	50
Rs. 201—300	48	12	15	54	129
Rs. 301—400	73	—	3	—	76
Rs. 401—500	—	—	—	1	1
No Response	3	99	30	3	135
Total	140	118	80	62	4

V

POLITICAL AFFILIATION

Distribution of heads by the political affiliation

Slum/ Party	No Affi- liation	Shiv Sena	Con- gress (I)	Janata	CPM	CPI	Others
Bharat Nagar	105	0	26	8	0	0	1
Hanuman Tekdi	66	4	39	8	0	1	0
Golibar	44	6	14	10	1	1	4
Worli	52	2	2	1	0	0	5
Total	267	12	81	27	1	2	10

VI

EVICTION PROCESS
on Eviction (Bharat Nagar)

Question	Yes	No	No Response
Have you got rent receipts?	132	3	5
Have you got a photo-pass ?	73	59	8
Do you know that owning a photo-pass does not make you permanent ? ..	2	125	13
Have the local authorities told you that a photo-pass makes you permanent ?..	1	125	14
Have you heard of the Vacant Land Act ?	1	125	14
Do you know that as per the Vacant Land Act all slums are temporary ..	75	48	17
Do you know that only 30 days' notice is necessary for demolition ? ..	48	75	17

Question	Yes	No	No Response
Do you know that courts are powerless to prevent demolition ? ..	108	15	17
Do you know that armed police can be used to demolish huts ?	108	15	17
Do you know that police atrocities cannot be questioned in court ? ..	84	39	17
Do you know that the money you paid is not a rent but a 'fine' ?	8	115	17
Do you know that part of the money you pay (as fine) is used for your eviction?	2	121	~17

Question	No money	Do not want to pay	Not applicable
Why don't you pay the rent ('fine') regularly?	127	9	4

Question	No Response
Did you pay any bribe to any local authorities ..	140

The reasons given for the Eviction

In the name of improvement	27
In the name of building new roads and widening old ones	46
In the name of constructing sanitary blocks	3
No response	64

Question	Yes	No	No Response
Did you want to move to the new place ?	28	79	33
Could you justify the reasons put forward by the Government for eviction ?	43	69	28

| Question | Yes | | No |
	Verbal	Written	Response
Were you told in writing or verbally that you would be given an alternative place or accommodation ?	8	86	46

Attitude of the Police during the eviction ?

Abused housewife	2
Disconnected electric line	1
Unfavourable	101
No Response	36

Attitude of the Tehsilder/Bill Collector during the eviction ?

Abused wife	1
Promised alternative arrangement	3
Helpless attitude	1
Faith in Government	1
Unfavourable	1
No Response	133

| Question | Yes | | No |
	Verbal	Written	
Were you given notice of eviction ?	7	97	36

Question	1 month	2 months	No Response
How many days' notice were you given ?	73	24	43

Question	Upto Rs. 100/-	More than Rs. 100	No Response
Money paid during eviction?	2	16	122

Question	Yes	No	Not Applicable/ No Response
Did you get any receipts for the money you paid ?	18	—	122

	Yes	No
Did you oppose the eviction ?	26	144

How did you oppose the eviction?

Conducted a morcha	24
No Response	2
Not Applicable	114

How did the Government react to your protests?

Tried to suppress	20
Bribed some dwellers	4
No Response	2
Not Applicable	114

When were you evicted?

1970	1
1971	2
1973	1
1974	9
1975	93
No Response	34

Comparison	Old and New Slums (i.e., before and after eviction)		
	Better	Same	Worse
Nearness to place of work ..	6	19	55
Safety of women ..	6	20	55
Water supply ..	12	15	55
Roads ..	6	7	65
Nearness to the Post Office ..	5	7	66
Latrines ..	3	16	63
Nearness to school ..	3	16	63
Nearness to hospitals ..	3	14	65
Playground ..	4	14	63
Quality of house ..	3	24	55
Electric supply ..	12	31	62
Nearness of caste/community ..	18	61	28
Nearness of people from same home town ..	20	64	23
Co-operation from neighbours ..	21	64	22

Tables on
Profile of Women in Slum

I

Distribution of women by religion

Hindu	Muslim	Christian	Neo-Buddhists	Total
52	16	—	30	100

Distribution of women by caste

Scheduled Caste	Scheduled Tribe	O.B.C.	Others	Total
28	—	11	61	100

Distribution of women by the occupation of their parents

Till own land	Land-less labou-rer	Handi-craft worker	Fac-tory wor-ker	Busi-ness	White collar job	Others	No res-ponse
13	17	1	9	3	4	2	51

Distribution of women by whether they worked during childhood

Worked	Did not work	No response
16	68	16

Distribution of women by their level of schooling

Nil	Lower Primary	Upper Primary	High School	S.S.C.	Graduation	No Response
10	22	21	1	3	2	41

Distribution of women by their reading habits

Newspapers	Books	Magazines	Others	Do not Read	Not Applicable (Illiterate)	No Response
9	19	6	4	12	7	43

Distribution of women by the reasons for moving to the slum

Accommodation problem	Unemployment	Troubles	After marriage	Did not like the old place	No response
16	14	1	35	23	11

Distribution of women by the age at their marriage

11—15 years	16—25 years	No response
50	35	15

Distribution of women by whether they gave dowry

Gave dowry	Did not give dowry	No response
24	69	7

Distribution of women by the amount given as dowry

Re. 1-500	Rs. 501-1000	Rs. 1001-2000	Rs. 2001-3000	Rs. 3001-5000	Rs. 5000-8000	Not applicable	No response
4	3	5	2	4	1	69	12

Distribution of women by the source from which money was borrowed (to be given as dowry)

Private Banking Institutions	No response	Not applicable
9	22	69

Distribution of women by the rate of interest on the borrowings

10 per cent	40 per cent	Without interest	Not applicable	No Response
4	1	4	69	22

Distribution of women by their martial status

Separated	Divorced	Widowed	Living together (married)	No response
1	3	6	67	23

Women X whethe∶ planning to remarry ?

Yes	No	Not applicable	No response
2	3	67	28

Women X Has your husband other women besides you?

Yes	No	No response
5	2	93

Women X Is it with your consent that your husband is keeping other women?

Yes	No	Not applicable
—	5	95

Whether there are any prostitutes in the slum

Yes	No response
77	23

Reasons for prostitution

To earn more money	For mere fun	Due to poverty	Due to illiteracy	Due to compulsion	No Response
54	3	16	1	3	23

Women X How often do you fight?

	Over mo- ney	Over dri- nks	Over wo- men	Over in- laws	Over wife's acti- vities	Others	No res- ponse
Do not fight	48	—	—	—	—	—	—
Often	14	—	—	1	—	1	1
Very often	10	13	3	3	1	3	1

Women X Husband's drinking habits

Does not drink 87	Drinks 13

Distribution of women by the number of children

Number of Children	One	Two	Three	Four	Five	Not speci- fied/No response
Male	24	25	14	9	2	
Female	37	16	14	5	—	16

Distribution of women by their views on family planning

Question	Yes	No	No response
Whether practised family planning	33	51	16
Whether practising now ?	23	61	16
Whether planning to have more children	17	65	18

Distribution of women by the number of children they want to have more

One	Two	Three	Not applicable/ No response
14	2	1	83

Distribution of women by the place where their children were delivered

Hospital	Home	No response
59	25	16

Women X Who attended them at the time of delivery

Doctor	Mid-wife	Others	No response
60	14	10	16

Whether the women had any special foods during pregnancy?

Yes	No	No response
67	2	31

The place where the women used to keep their children when they work?

Home	Creches	School	Friend's Place	In-laws' Place	Not Applicable/ No Response
43	0	6	1	2	48

Distribution of women by whether they send their children to school

Yes	No	No Response
17	67	16

Whether the women used to beat their child?

Yes	No	No Response
66	23	11

III

Decision-makers in the family

	Number of children	Marriages (of children)	Schooling	Household budget	Entertainments	Other household matters	No Response
Husband	30	31	34	34	34	30	3
Wife	25	17	17	18	17	12	3
Both	42	49	49	48	49	55	3

Distribution of women by their views on household matters etc.

Question	Yes	No
Women should look after home ?	82	18
Both men and women should do house-work?	59	41
House-work is boring	18	82
House-work is too heavy	19	81
All women should have children ?	95	5
There should be common creches ?	79	21
Only the mother can really look after the child ?	82	18

Women should spend their full time on children ?	71	29
Child would not develop if it is with the mother all the time ?	40	60
If man earns enough, women need not work ? ..	67	33
Women should work because it will give her independence ?	24	76
Women should have equal rights as men ?	82	18
Women's first duty is to do house-work ? ..	86	14
Men should also care for 'children'	85	15
Women should get less pay ?	36	64
Women can work as efficiently as men ?	85	15
Education is essential for male and female children ?	96	4
Men are superior ?	86	14
Men are more privileged ?	91	9
Wife should obey her husband ?	69	31
There should be no dowry system ?	68	32
Family planning is good ?	93	7
Everybody should practise family planning	93	7
There should be a boy child in every family ..	87	13
There is nothing wrong in abortion ?	58	42
Abortion should be free in Bombay ?	73	27

Number of women by hours of work spent on household works

Hours/Job	Cleaning	Cooking	Child Care	Miscellaneous
1 hour	80	81	81	83
2-3 hours	7	6	6	6
4-5 hours	1	3	1	1
6+ hours	1	1	1	1

Women by their employment status

Employed	Unemployed	No response
56	33	11

Type of employment of the women

Domestic	Factory	Given to do at home	Others
40	9	1	6

Women X Employment Profiles

Questions	Yes	No	Not applicable/ No response
Worked daily ?	49	7	0
Hours of work fixed ?	21	33	2
Breaks were available ?	16	38	2
Medical care provided ?	6	8	42
Canteen was provided ?	5	9	42
Insurance facilities ?	3	12	41
Sick leave was granted ?	10	44	2
Creches were provided ?	2	12	42
Lighter work for women ?	2	11	43
Maternity leave granted ?	7	42	7

Distribution of women by the present wage X First wage from the present job

Present / First	Re. 1—100	Rs. 101—200	Rs. 201—300	Rs. 301—400
Re 1—100	26	3	—	—
Rs. 101—200	6	6	—	—
Rs. 201—300	4	2	2	—
Rs. 301—400	1	1	—	1

Distribution of women by property owned by them of their family

Land	Shop	House	Jewellery (Gold & Silver)	Not applicable (i.e., No property owned)	No Response
30	8	17	31	4	10

Distribution of women by whether the land owned yielded any income

Land yields income	Land does not yield any income	Not applicable
15	15	70

V

Amenities not available (Response of the women)

Water	Electricity	Sanitation	Lavatory	Gas
95	72	85	90	3

Do you have ration and milk card ?

	Ration Card	Milk Card
Yes	78	29
No	22	71

INDEX